THE PRENATAL THEME
IN PSYCHOTHERAPY

THE PRENATAL THEME
IN PSYCHOTHERAPY

Philippe Ployé

Foreword by
Alessandra Piontelli

KARNAC
LONDON   NEW YORK

First published in 2006 by
H. Karnac (Books) Ltd.
6 Pembroke Buildings, London NW10 6RE

Copyright © 2006 by The Estate of Philippe Ployé
Foreword copyright © 2006 by Alessandra Piontelli

The rights of Philippe Ployé to be identified as the author of this work have been asserted in accordance with §§ 77 and 78 of the Copyright Design and Patents Act 1988.

All rights reserved. No part of this publication may be reproduced, stored in a retrieval system, or transmitted, in any form or by any means, electronic, mechanical, photocopying, recording, or otherwise, without the prior written permission of the publisher.

British Library Cataloguing in Publication Data

A C.I.P. for this book is available from the British Library

ISBN-13: 978-1-85575-364-8
ISBN-10: 1-85575-364-2

Edited, designed, and produced by Communication Crafts

Printed in Great Britain

www.karnacbooks.com

CONTENTS

ACKNOWLEDGEMENTS vii

FOREWORD by Alessandra Piontelli ix

Introduction 1

1   Review of the literature 5

2   Clinical material 39

3   The placenta and its possible role in ego development 87

4   Notes on placental symbolism 101

5   Additional remarks about the literature concerned with prenatal life 115

REFERENCES 145

INDEX 161

ACKNOWLEDGEMENTS

In addition to my gratitude to the late Dr T. F. Main, without whose Directorship my old hospital would not have provided the setting I needed to do the work I was interested in, I should like to extend this gratitude to all those colleagues who, whether by sending me complimentary copies of their books or reprints or offprints of their papers, or giving me encouragement and expressing interest generally, have been of such help to me. It is a long list. I have done my best to mention everyone, and they are:

The late Prof. D. Anzieu, Prof. J. Bicknell, the late Dr O. H. D. Blomfield, Dr D. Brown, Dr M. Chiesa, the late Prof. G. Devereux, Mr L. DeMause, the late Dr F. Dolto, Dr W. E. Freud, the late Dr A. Garma, the late Dr G. H. Graber, Dr B. Grunberger, the late Dr P. Heimann, Dr D. Kelsey, the late Mr M. Khan, Dr F. Kruse, Dr R. Langs, the late Dr M. Lietaert Peerbolte, Dr S. Maiello, Dr J. Mitrani, the late Mr F. J. Mott, Dr E. Osterweil, Dr M. I. Paul, Dr A. Piontelli, Prof. J. Raphael-Leff, Dr A. Rascovsky, Dr D. I. Rushton, Dr J. Sarkissoff, Mr C. Sacerdoti, the late Dr W. Clifford M. Scott, Dr L. Share, Dr N. Symington, the late Mrs F. Tustin, and Dr J. Wilheim.

My thanks also go the Library Staff of the Institute of Psycho-Analysis in London, and to all the various secretaries without whose help, especially in the case of Mrs Jane Winder and Mrs Annie Benbow, this book would never have seen the light of day.

Finally, I should like to take this opportunity to pay tribute to the memory of Sir Ernest Cassel [1852–1921], to whose generosity my old hospital owes both its foundation and its name, and the support of whose descendants this hospital has continued to enjoy to this day. The present book owes almost everything to experience obtained from working with inpatients or outpatients referred to the Cassel Hospital between 1948 and 1981.

FOREWORD

Alessandra Piontelli

Several months ago Dr Philippe Ployé asked me to write a short foreword for his manuscript, and he was very keen to see his great effort published. Sadly this book sees the light posthumously.

The Prenatal Theme in Psychotherapy is a multilayered work.

First of all, Dr Ployé's own personality emerges as you read the book. In all his clinical examples, he comes across as a very attentive, respectful, and devoted psychoanalyst, who listens carefully to his patients and questions and mulls over his interpretations, showing remarkable honesty and modesty in discussing his achievements as well as his failures in trying to understand.

All his clinical examples deal with a particular form of transference that could be called the prenatal or the foetal transference. Highly disturbed patients seem to be stuck forever in a foetal mode, while well-functioning or less disturbed ones can go through transitory shifts into this particular state of mind.

Dr Ployé meticulously describes the prenatal mode of operating, characterized by extreme dependency on the analyst and intense passivity. The patient withdraws inside his or her mental cocoon and expects the analyst to function as an idealized placenta or umbilical cord would, by providing everything effortlessly and without having to scream, struggle, or ask. The analyst, perceived as an extension of her/himself, functions as an auxiliary ego. Extreme parasitism as well as concrete thinking characterize this particular mode. The idealized uterus is both protective and threatening, making the patient at times feel trapped and persecuted by its tight mental cocoon.

Dr Ployé's description of the prenatal state of mind is both convincing and illuminating and can alert all of us to the functioning of this particular mode.

Finally, Dr Ployé examines the thinking of all his predecessors and contemporaries who have talked about foetal life. In addition to further enriching his description of the foetal mode of mental functioning, this detailed review certainly has historical value. However, reading the work of all these thinkers makes one realize just how impossible it is to reconstruct prenatal life from transference, as the theories that emerge from the consulting-room are far-fetched and often unbalanced and have little to do with the reality of prenatal life. Foetal transference and any subsequent interpretations associated with it should only be taken as apt metaphors. Dr Ployé was cautiously aware of this, but perhaps too modest to openly spell it out.

Introduction

This book is an attempt to examine a question that has already aroused the interest of an increasing number of psychoanalysts and psychotherapists: whether patients in analysis or therapy can sometimes be said to form a kind of transference that not only operates at prenatal level but can also lend itself to interpretation just like any other (postnatal) level of transference.[1] Although the research carried out in the course of the last fifty years or so has shown that the foetus's ability to feel, experience, and perceive is much more developed than one had previously thought, there is still some understandable doubt as to whether it is capable of feeling fear or aggression, of distinguishing between itself and its environment—that is, between "self" and "non-self"; and hence whether the prenatal condition, usually conceived from a psychological point of view as one of objectless, pre-ambivalent fusion with the mother, would be capable of being relived and re-enacted later in the form of a object-directed, aggressive, as well as libidinal, "foetal" form of relatedness to the therapist. Even if a patient appeared to be relating psychologically to the therapist in a way that bore a striking resemblance to the way in which the foetus relates to the mother physically, it would probably be argued—again understandably—that what was being seen was in fact nothing more than a composite kind of transference in which a truly object-directed, aggressive, as well as libidinal *postnatal* form or level of relatedness was being perceived against the backdrop of a vague memory of having been in the womb, thus producing the illusion of a foetal, object-directed, aggressive, and libidinal form of transference.

I am only too aware of how difficult it is to know what a foetus or even an embryo really feels. All I can say—and I do my best to illustrate this by means of clinical material—is that one may sometimes come across patients who relate to the therapist *as if* they—or at least parts of themselves—were reliving and re-enacting a foetal level of relatedness that, apart from its foetal features, does not appear to be fundamentally different from any other postnatal, object-directed, aggressive as well as libidinal form of transference. (The notion of foetal aggressivity is discussed in the course of the work.)

The greatest difficulty of all, it seems to me—and one that is also mentioned several times in the course of this work—is not that of making educated guesses as to what could be our earliest forms of experience, or even that of finding words to describe these: it is the difficulty of communicating our "findings", if such they are, to our patients in a way that helps them by meaning something to them. It may satisfy our scientific curiosity and search for truth to feel or think we understand a little better than before how postnatal mental life and behaviour could be influenced by the continued effect on them of what we believe to be these earliest and as yet "unmentalized"[2] forms of experience; but patients often respond to such reconstructions with something like: "But how does this help me?", "What shall I do with it?", or "It doesn't get me anywhere". One way of dealing with this difficulty—another is mentioned below—seems to be to bear in mind that even when the particular wording of a patient's communication appears to call for an interpretation on prenatal lines, a little more reflection will nearly always show that an interpretation on postnatal lines would also have been possible and would also have made more sense to the patient, and that, from a *therapeutic* point of view, it would really be more helpful to offer the "postnatal" interpretation first, the question of whether to complement it with the "prenatal" one, either at the time or later, being for the therapist to decide.

The term "foetal transference" was, I think, used for the first time by Symington (1981, p. 195). The words themselves invite the question of whether the countertransference, too, can sometimes be seen to operate at pre/or perinatal level—that is, whether the therapist can either experience, or even act out in his or her countertransference, the reactions that the patient's mother may have gone through—and may later sometimes be revealed as having actually gone through—during her pregnancy or labour.

In the case of inpatients, such countertransferences sometimes appear capable of being acted out by a whole therapeutic team. The material presented by Patient A gives examples of one of those moments when a transference appears to justify its being interpreted on prenatal lines, and of what could also be regarded as one of these "puerperal" or "prepuerperal" forms of countertransference. Patient C also provided material that seemed to have responded to interpretations offered on prenatal lines, but her unresolved prenatal drive does not seem to have affected the countertransference as it did in the case of Patient A.

Some of the material provided by Patient A in particular having made me realize the possible relevance, to postnatal psychology, of the fact that we relate to the prenatal mother by means of a part of ourselves that we then lose at birth—namely our erstwhile placenta—I shall be adding a few extra thoughts on the subject in the form of two short chapters, one about the role that the placenta could be conceived to play in the formation of the ego, and the other giving a list of possible placenta symbols, together with a short note about Freud's thoughts concerning heredity.

The book ends with some additional remarks about the literature concerning the prenatal stage. It may unfortunately not be strictly up-to-date.

NOTES

1. *Transference* and *countertransference* are major psychoanalytic concepts. "Transference" refers to the fact that the way we relate to others is often seen to reflect some of the patterns of behaviour we have developed over the years as a result of the influence brought to bear upon us by our parents, educators, the society we live in, and indeed our own nature. These patterns are so to

speak "transferred" on to those around us. The patient "transfers" them onto the analyst, and the latter, in what is described as his or her "countertransference", transfers his or her own patterns onto the patient. The successful outcome of a psychoanalytically based form of therapy often involves a better appreciation and understanding by both parties of the way they have reacted to each other.

    2. The word is taken from chapters 6 and 10 of Mitrani's book *A Framework for the Imaginary* (1996).

CHAPTER ONE

Review of the literature

> ... and it would be foolish to believe that the mind begins to function only at the moment of birth.
>
> Sándor Ferenczi (1913, p. 219)

I would have liked to include in this review[1] the several references that Freud himself made, in the course of his writings, to the prenatal phase and also some of Abraham's own references to it (e.g. 1913, p. 205), but I felt it might be in order to concentrate on the writings of those authors who, in the way they have referred to the prenatal phase, can be seen to have considered the possibility that foetal modes of functioning and relating can sometimes be repeated in the way that patients relate to the analyst or the therapist, and that the material that they produce on those occasions can therefore be interpreted, not simply as the product or expression of a mere "phantasy", but as the actual re-living and reproduction, *in the transference,* of a prenatal mode of relating and experience: in other words, that just as patients sometimes appear to be treating and relating to the therapist as if the latter were, say, an unconsciously remembered and re-experienced maternal breast, so they can also sometimes be said to treat and relate to him as if he were their erstwhile placenta, or an unconsciously remembered and re-experienced womb and inside of the mother's body.

The idea is by no means new. Ferenczi (1913) was, I think, the first to point out that the material produced by patients in analysis sometimes refers, without the patient being aware of this, to the latter's experience of prenatal life.

Rank considered that certain transferences could be regarded as reproducing, at least at one level, the "physiological connection" that had existed between the mother and her unborn child (1924, pp. 5–6). He also drew attention to the fact that legends, myths, patients' associations, and so on often contained what appeared to be symbolic references to the act and experience of birth. His paper on the birth "trauma" (1924) was a landmark in psychoanalytic literature, but he made what is now generally acknowledged to have been the mistake of making the working through of this particular "trauma" the central point of his whole technique, thus not only exaggerating the importance of birth in relation to other factors, but also leaving little room for the possibility that being born might also be a welcome "liberation" from adverse prenatal conditions (DeMause, 1982, p. 251)—a little like the break of dawn after a troubled night.

The year 1924—that is, the year of publication of Rank's book on the birth trauma and its relevance to postnatal psychology— also saw the first of a series of publications of a Swiss analyst, the late Dr G. H. Graber, who in 1971 was to found a study group that then developed into the International Association for Prenatal Psychology (Internationale Studiengemeinschaft für Pränatale Psychologie, or ISPP). This latter Association, which in 1986 became the International Society for Prenatal and Perinatal Psychology and Medicine (ISPPPM), today has many branches all over the world.[2] Another society, called the Pre- and Perinatal Psychology Association of North America (PPANA), founded by Dr T. Verny (W. E. Freud, personal communication), and an even more recent study group resulted in the foundation in 1991 of the Brazilian Association for the Study of Pre- and Perinatal Psychism (ABREP—the initials being, of course, those of the Portuguese name), by a Brazilian psychoanalyst, Dr Joanna Wilheim, and some of her colleagues (see other references to Wilheim below).

Simmel (1929) observed that when patients were treated "by psychoanalysis" in a hospital environment, the "psychoanalytic situation"—by which he obviously meant the "transference"—was not "restricted to the relations between analysand and analyst" but included "the whole clinic as a kind of extension of the analyst's personality or as an archetype of the family in general" (p. 79); "the matron and attendants [represented] the mother, the physician the father, the fellow-patients (and sometime the nurses too), the brothers and sisters". He also pointed out, however, that patients treated by psychoanalysis in this environment tended to "identify their life in the clinic, protected as they [were] by the analysis, with the hidden intra-uterine existence" (p. 86) and that this created a "special kind of resistance" (p. 87). Like Rank, therefore, Simmel seems to have suggested the existence, as well as the interpretability, of prenatal levels of transference.

Balint (1937) described what he called the stage of "archaic" or "primary object-love", held by him to be the "very earliest stage of extra-uterine mental life" (p. 103)—an interesting phrase that suggests some agreement with Ferenczi's belief (1913, p. 219) in the possibility of some degree of intra-uterine mental life. According to Balint, the attempt by certain patients to recreate in their sessions the experience of "primary object-love" involved the search for a "love" that was not an "oral, oral-sucking, anal, genital, etc." kind of love, but "something on its own" (1937, p. 101); it aspired to a "tranquil, quiet sense of well-being" (pp. 98, 102). It could be regarded as object-directed because its withdrawal brought forth instantaneous and "extremely violent reactions" and "insatiable cravings" reminiscent of addiction (p. 102) or of the "very noisy, dramatic and vehement" reactions produced by the sudden interruption of air supply—that is, by the withdrawal of the object "air" (1951, p. 145). As Balint rightly pointed out, air supply was something we normally took for granted, and in the same way as we can hardly see "any signs of satisfaction" when "the need for air is gratified" (p. 145), so satisfied primary object-love, too, is "silent", almost impossible to detect since all we see is the "state of quiet, tranquil well-being" (p. 144). This dependence on the object air (the underlining of which was in my opinion long overdue in psychoanalytic literature and theory), as well as his several references to "addiction" or "addiction-like states" (1935, p. 193; 1937, pp. 97, 102; 1952, p. 246), were Balint's way of illustrating what he considered to be the other main characteristic of primary object-love, namely its "almost *absolute dependence* on the object" (1951, p. 145; emphasis in original).

Now, as Graber pointed out (1972, pp. 60–61), Balint's description of what he conceived as satisfied "primary object-love" is very evocative of what one could imagine to be the "silent" and "quiet" state of intra-uterine "well-being" if the pregnancy is a happy and normal one. The stage of prenatal "love", too, is, moreover, characterized by an "absolute", life-and-death sort of "dependence on an object", namely the body of a mother on whom the unborn child depends for an uninterrupted supply of oxygen and nutrients and for also having its wastes immediately and continuously disposed of. Furthermore, prenatal "love" itself could be said to be "not oral, oral-sucking, anal, genital, etc.", but "something on its own".

Balint does not, however, appear to have considered for very long the possibility of equating the search for "primary object-love" with the search for prenatal or uterine "love"; he seems, in fact, to have decided against it. The reason for this seems to have had something to do with what both he and Ferenczi had felt to be the ineffectiveness, when a patient showed some difficulty in achieving a complete "surrender" of himself "in love or in treatment", of telling the patient that although the latter probably wished to regress "to the mother's womb", he was also afraid to do so lest coming out of the regression would mean a traumatic birth all over again. Both Ferenczi and Balint had observed that such interpretations, although readily accepted by patients, "hardly touched them emotionally" (Balint, 1935, p. 71). This seems to have been the reason why Balint, although recognizing the similarity between the state of "primary object-love" and the prenatal state, eventually gave up interpreting what he called the "colourless 'regression to the mother's womb'", feeling such interpretations to be "unreal" and "phantastic" compared to the vividness of affects "called forth" by interpretations that addressed not only the wish, but also the reluctance, to surrender to "passive" or "primary object-love".[3] I cannot, of course, be sure of this, but I would imagine that when these words were written, analysts' comments to their patients about "regression to the mother's womb" would have said little if anything about the possible existence of foetal forms of "transference", foetal "aggressivity", or the wish to live inside the analyst in a parasitical, destructive, object-seeking and object-related sort of way. If so, this could perhaps explain what Balint reported as the failure of his and Ferenczi's interpretations to "touch" patients "emotionally", or the lack of "colour" he complained about. Notwithstanding this, I think it quite likely that Balint's description of frustrated "primary object-love" may eventually come to be seen as an unwitting description of frustrated intra-uterine "love".

Marie Bonaparte (1938) wrote that although she had "no desire to endow the cells with a psychology" (p. 215), she wondered whether the fear that certain women have of being "penetrated, perforated or ripped open" by the male could be the reactivation of some sort of protoplasmic memory of having been perforated or broken into, as an ovum, by the sperm at conception (p. 214).[4] She also wondered whether certain castration fears in males could go back to the sperm's biological experience of protoplasmic "disintegration" and "loss of substance" within the ovum after penetration (p. 216). She thus appears to have been thinking in terms of destructive forces operating at the biochemical level during conception. Other writers—Fodor (1951), Lietaert Peerbolte, (1975, pp. 24–41, 293–294), and, more recently, Wilheim (1988)—have considered this possibility since then.

Karl Menninger (1939) pointed out that if we were to accept Freud's notion of a life instinct the aim of which is to build and of a death instinct the aim of which is to destroy, it would be illogical and inconsistent to make an exception of prenatal life and declare the latter to be conflict-free: "if living and dying, construction and destruction, loving and hating deserve the appellation of instincts, and are to be regarded as fundamental and universal, we are logically obliged to conceive of them as operating in some way within the personality of the unborn child" (p. 440).

Accordingly, Menninger suggested that "at the time of fertilization the self-destructive tendencies of both male and female parents [were] temporarily overcome [by their union] . . . with the result that a tremendous impulse [was] given to the life instinct drives of the new individual". Although the sentences that follow do not say this explicitly, I get the impression that they can be interpreted as Menninger's proposal that after the union of the gametes thus "neutralizes" for a while their respective death instincts,[5] the foetus is then protected from its own death instinct "by the influence of the surrounding maternal body"; and that although its self-destructive impulses temporarily re-emerge at birth with the separation from this body, they are once again "more or less neutralized" by their deflection on to the postnatal mother and the support given by her.

In that same 1939 paper, Menninger quoted extracts from a 1937 article by Devereux on the beliefs of certain primitive Indian tribes concerning the "psychology" of the unborn child; his interest in that article seems to me to confirm that his hypothesis came very near to including a notion according to which the embryo and foetus would also be conceived as averting the threat of their self-directed destructive impulses (death instinct) by deflecting these, *in utero*, on the inside of the mother's body. In other words, Menninger seems to me to have come very close to formulating the hypothesis of a prenatal, object-seeking and object-related form of aggressivity that is directed at the inside of the mother's body from within.

Greenacre (1941, 1945) is well known for her pioneering work on the mother–foetus relationship and for raising the question of whether the foetus's reactivity to certain—presumably unpleasant—stimuli could be regarded as what she called a "pre-anxiety" kind of response. If we accept Melanie Klein's view that anxiety results from the ego's fear that it will be annihilated by its own destructive impulses unless it can deflect these outwards onto something or someone else (1946, p. 298), acceptance of Greenacre's notion of a prenatal precursor of anxiety would presumably necessitate including that of a prenatal precursor of aggressivity such as "pre-aggressivity". Clifford Scott (1949, p. 144), Winnicott (1949, p. 141), and, later, Money-Kyrle (1968, p. 692 n.3), to quote but a few, have also expressed their own interest in the prenatal phase and in the possible usefulness of further research into this field.

Fodor (1949, 1951, 1962) is acknowledged by several writers as one of the pioneers in the field of prenatal research, particularly with respect to his use of dreams (1951) as a means of reconstructing prenatal experience and events. He seems to have been responsible for having introduced the term "conception shock". As we saw, Marie Bonaparte had suggested the possibility of such a "shock" as far back as 1936, although without using the same word. Fodor was also interested in the possible relevance of foetal modes of awareness to parapsychological phenomena.

Lietaert Peerbolte (1951, 1952, 1975, pp. 42–54) may well have been the first to suggest the possible existence of placenta "symbols" and hence the possibility, when such presumed symbols appear in damaged form in patients' material, of reconstructing cases where prenatal suffering had been caused or contributed to by placental defect, malfunction, or injury. In addition to being interested, as mentioned earlier, in the possibility of "conception shock" (1975, pp. 24–41, 134–144, 185, 293–294), Lietaert Peerbolte, like Fodor, was also interested in the possible relevance of foetal modes of awareness to parapsychological phenomena. In the second half of his book, *Psychic Energy* (1975), he gives a list of Fodor's publications concerned with parapsychology and psychoanalysis (p. 265).

Mott's extensive research into the prenatal symbolism contained in dreams (1948, 1959, 1964) and in myths (1960) should be of great interest to anyone engaged in psychoanalytic or psychotherapeutic work. His whole work is a thorough-going study of what he regarded as the prenatal foundations of the postnatal human "mind", and his research into what he, too, believed to be instances of placental symbolism has been of great help in stimulating my own interest in the subject.

Melanie Klein (1952a, p. 263) wrote in a footnote that "recent studies of prenatal modes of behaviour" (she quoted in this respect Gesell's 1945 book, *Embryology of Behaviour*) provided food for thought about the existence of a "rudimentary ego . . . already at work in the foetus". (See also below for a more detailed reference to Klein's 1957 volume, as well as to her work in general.)

Kelsey (1953) uncovered what he described as unconscious memories of conception or of prenatal life in his treatment of certain patients by hypnoanalysis.

Evans (1955) presented material from the analysis of a boy in the latency period which not only showed the latter's unconscious awareness of the umbilical cord and the way it had connected him with his mother's body, but also her own awareness of the light that the boy's twisting of some string to form a rope appeared to shed on the connection and relationship he had formed to other people, including herself (pp. 63–64).

A. Rascovsky too, like Melanie Klein, expressed his belief (1956) in the possible usefulness of conceiving of a rudimentary ego that would already be at work *in utero*. He made an interesting reference to the Greek legend in which Ulysses and his companions owe their escape from the cave to the fact that Ulysses manages to blind the one-eyed giant Polyphemus who guards it. If I have understood him rightly, Rascovsky saw the blinding of this cyclopean eye—or "I"—as a symbolic allusion to the way in which the "prenatal nucleus of the ego and the characteristics of its vision" must first be "superseded" and left behind at birth before the individual can fully emerge from the uterine "cave" into the outside world (p. 286). I have asked myself whether this prenatal, cyclopean "eye" or "I", notwithstanding Rascovsky's suggestion concerning its possible "phylogenetic" origins (p. 288), could also be susceptible to a "placental" interpretation, according to which a placental "eye"—or "I"—would be conceived as "looking into" the inside of the mother's body, and as being itself "killed" at birth. (Regarding this possible placental interpretation of the prenatal "eye" or "I", chapter three suggests the possibility of making some kind of link between the functions of the placenta and those of the postnatal ego. See also below for further reference to the work of Rascovsky and his collaborators.)

Mahler, Pine, and Bergman (1975) have contributed much to our understanding of the almost constant overlap into postnatal life and behaviour of prenatal modes of functioning and relating, and hence to our awareness of the importance of interpreting such overlap in the transference whenever appropriate.

In one of her later works (1957, p. 179), Melanie Klein wrote that "how far [the prenatal state] is undisturbed must depend on the condition of the mother and possibly on certain unexplored factors in the unborn infant"; and that "unpleasant experiences" *in utero*, "together with the feeling of security in the womb", may precede and "foreshadow" the postnatal good breast/bad breast type of dichotomy.

It seems reasonable to suppose that by "unpleasant experiences" Klein was referring to the kind of events she described as giving rise to what she called "persecutory anxiety". We also know that she saw such "anxiety" as the ego's fear of being overwhelmed or annihilated by the self-directed aggressivity of its own death instinct (1948, pp. 278–279) and that, in agreement with Freud, she held that the ego dealt with this threat by deflecting this self-directed aggressivity onto other objects or people in the form of outwardly directed aggression. This, coupled with what I referred to above as her interest in the conceivability of a rudimentary prenatal ego (1952a, p. 263n), may justify speculating about how her thinking might have proceeded from there had she lived a few years longer. Since she was beginning to think in terms of a possible good womb/bad womb type of dichotomy, would she, too, like Karl Menninger, have gone on to consider the possible usefulness of not only postulating the existence of destructive impulses operating *in utero*, but of also extending her theoretical framework by making the womb, or the prenatal mother, the first "object" of all aggressive and libidinal strivings?[6] Whatever answer we may choose to give to this question, I cannot help thinking that the emphasis placed by Melanie Klein on the drive to get inside the mother's body, drain it dry, excrete into it, and so on may eventually cause her to be seen as having intuitively adumbrated, and in effect described, what further research may be able to tell us about the overlap, into postnatal oral and anal mechanisms, of what certain writers are beginning to envisage as the aggressive aspects of the prenatal drive.

As one of these writers—Paul (1983, pp. 562–563), of whom more later—has clearly implied, the phantasies that Melanie Klein described may be nothing less than the continuation, in postnatal life and psychological form, of what was once a physiological reality. Klein described the infant as emptying excreta into the mother's breast and body *in phantasy*, but the unborn child empties its wastes into her body *in reality*. Going back, therefore, to what I said earlier about Balint's description of what he called the stage of "primary object-love", it could be asked whether he and Melanie Klein will both eventually be seen—assuming the validity of some of the ideas presented here—as having adumbrated much of what future research may be able to tell us about both the aggressive (Klein) and the libidinal (Balint) components of the prenatal drive, respectively.

Garma (1958, 1966, 1970, 1974) has contributed much to our understanding of how certain dreams contain hidden references to prenatal life and events.

Influenced by the work of Dolto (1981a, 1981b), Bernard This wrote an interesting and well-informed chapter on prenatal life in his book *La Psychanalyse* (1960).

Bion (1965, p. 28) gave a detailed description of certain "parasitical" forms of transference in which the patient phantasies himself as living inside the analyst and in which the aggressivity involved takes the form of actively destroying every "link" the analyst tries to establish, either between the patient's conscious and unconscious processes or between the latter's past (or present) reactions to other people and the here-and-now aspects of his relatedness to the analyst himself (1959). As I have recalled elsewhere (Ployé, 1984), the idea that the foetus can be likened to a parasite can be found not only in the writings of biologists and embryologists (see my quotation from Hamilton and Mossman below)—but also in those of Ferenczi (1913, p. 218; 1933–1934), Deutsch (1947, p. 115), Mahler (1952, p. 286), and, more recently, Paul (1983), Grunberger (1983), Blomfield (1985, 1987), and quite possibly other publications I have not yet come across. In his description of the parasitical forms of transference, Bion admittedly focused his attention on the mainly postnatal—whether oral, anal, or urethral—nature of the aggressivity involved, but in his recorded and posthumously edited *Bion in New York and São Paulo* (1980) he made several references to prenatal life. He thought it "reasonable to suppose", for example, that the foetus and even the embryo had a "mind which one day could be described as highly" (p. 22) or "potentially" (p. 108) "intelligent", and he speculated about "when" the embryo could "be said to feel fear or aggression" (p. 78).

Bion (1980) also suggested that the mechanism described by Melanie Klein as "projective identification" could take place even before birth (pp. 104, 108);[7] he even went as far as wondering whether the foetus could sometimes be aware of "things" that were "not-self", like "sensations of light", "sensations of noise" (p. 27), or variations of "pressure . . . transmitted through the amniotic fluid" (p. 99). Reading this made me think that Bion may presumably have been prepared to include the possibility that the foetus could also have some rudimentary awareness of other "happenings" (Bion's word—1980, p. 99) or "events" such as, for example, fluctuations of pressure gradients brought about by variations in the mother's condition (relaxed or under stress, awake or asleep), or position (standing, sitting or lying down); movements of the mother's body; the sound of her voice, footsteps, and heartbeat; the chemical "aggression" of noxious substances like nicotine, alcohol, or drugs; reactions to parental intercourse; accidents such as the mother falling, attempts at abortion, and dozens of other such "happenings" that could all leave some kind of memory trace in the unconscious of the growing individual and be communicated about later in analysis or psychotherapy by means of the numerous and varied metaphors, images and symbols that constitute what could be called the "language" of prenatality.[8]

It could therefore be said that towards the end of his life, Bion was beginning to speculate in one way or another about the possible existence of prenatal, object-seeking, and parasitical forms of transference in which aggressivity would play a considerable part. By the same token, his repeated references to the "containing" analyst and the "contained" patient (1962, 1963) are almost an invitation to consider the interaction that may have taken place, during the prenatal life of a given patient, between the "containing" prenatal mother and the patient himself as the "contained" foetus or embryo. Later, Raphael-Leff herself was to mention (1992, p. 2) how in pregnancy the mother-to-be does in actuality fulfil a "container" function for her foetus, "providing nutrients and carrying away wastes, feeding, breathing, excreting and metabolizing for her baby with every pulse of her heart beat"; and as this same writer has also rightly pointed out, this notion of a prenatal mother "container" can be linked with "Bion's concept of the postnatal maternal container".

Veszy-Wagner (1966) wrote about the way in which the analyst's room can sometimes represent the inside of the mother's body—"both cornucopia and torture-chamber" (p. 18). I do not know whether she thought the foetus capable of having actually "experienced" the womb itself as sometimes "good" and sometimes "bad", but the above quotation suggests that she thought patients capable of forming a kind of "transference" to her room, even if not to her too: a transference which the patient would then—presumably once again—experience as either "good" or "bad" according to whatever his or her disposition, and no doubt that of the analyst as well, happened to be at the time.

Milaković (1967, 1982, pp. 126–127) has described what he sees as a prenatal, "deglutitive" phase of libidinal development, and I shall refer to this notion again later when reporting the material of Patient C in chapter two.

A. Rascovsky (1971a, 1971b) and his collaborators seem to have interpreted prenatal levels of transference in their everyday clinical practice as early as in the 1960s, and I think it might also be true to say that in doing this they have been using the notion of prenatal aggressivity fairly consistently even if they did not refer to it under that name. Perhaps I can enlarge on both these points.

My impression that our South American colleagues can be said to have interpreted prenatal material within the transference is based on several points of their writings, but more particularly on a particular passage in a paper that describes the transference/countertransference interaction in the treatment of manic disorders (A. Rascovsky et al., 1971b). I should like to quote it here as relevant to my prenatal "theme", not only because Rascovsky and his collaborators have repeatedly expressed their opinion (for example, A. and M. Rascovsky, 1971a, pp. 28–29) that the omnipotent feeling and behaviour of manic patients is an attempt to recreate, as a defence against depression, what the authors see as the "omnipotence" of the foetal condition, but also because they quoted, in this connection (p. 28), Ferenczi's idea (1913, pp. 218–219) that the feeling of omnipotence could be traced back to the foetal feeling of having all instinctual demands completely satisfied all the time. The following passage from the 1971b paper by A. Rascovsky and others (on the transference and countertransference interaction in the treatment of manic disorders) may give some idea of how the authors responded to patients who showed signs of having regressed to a stage of foetal omnipotence. They describe (p. 178), for example, how manic patients sometimes act out this omnipotence by entering the analyst's office as if they owned the place, helping themselves to books on the shelves, looking at private papers, using the telephone, and so on, and how an interpretation of their manic defence then "liberates intense paranoid reactions", as if the "breaking of the manic defence is experienced as the cutting of a phantasied umbilical cord, resulting in the increase of persecutory and depressive anxiety" (translated by the author). This example alone seems to me to show that the patients' prenatal regression was interpreted within the transference, with the analyst's office being interpreted as some kind of phantasied womb.

That A. Rascovsky and his collaborators can probably also be said to have made use, when interpreting such transferences, of what I refer to here as the notion of prenatal aggressivity seems to me suggested by their frequent use of Kleinian concepts and terminology. As mentioned earlier, for example, Melanie Klein saw the infant as protecting itself from the potentially destructive effect of its death instinct by deflecting the latter outwards in the form of oral aggressivity directed between feeds at the mother's body and her absent breast, but Rascovsky and his colleagues saw this search for an "inexhaustible" breast as the continued search for what had been the uninterrupted umbilical "supply" (Rascovsky et al., 1971b, pp. 171–172). These writers do therefore seem to me to have come very near—as Menninger himself appears to have done—to regarding the prenatal phase as one in which the unborn child averts the potentially damaging effect of its death instinct by turning its aggressivity onto the inside of the mother's body *from within*. Finally, at the end of his 1956 paper on the "prenatal ego" (p. 289), A. Rascovsky wrote about the *"increase* of aggressivity provoked by the birth trauma" (emphasis added). The word "increase" seems another reason for saying that he had perhaps allowed for the possibility of some aggressivity having already been at work *in utero*.

Towards the end of his career, Graber also appears to have come to consider the conceivability of aggressivity operating before birth. For many years, and as can be seen in his earlier writings,[9] Graber had accepted the frequently held view that the prenatal condition was one that knew of no "splitting", "polarity", or "ambivalence" (1975, pp. 63–64), and that it was the separation from the mother at birth that introduced the first "hate" ["*Urhass*"] (p. 85), and with it the first split, the first polarity, and the first ambivalence (p. 84). Towards the end of his life, however, and influenced—like Greenacre and Melanie Klein before him—by the findings obtained from the direct observation of foetal behaviour, Graber began to question his earlier view that the prenatal phase was conflict-free. Not only did he begin to allow for the possibility of "unpleasant experiences" ["*Unlusterlebnisse*"] occurring *in utero* (1972, p. 38), but he even considered the possibility, in certain cases, of some sort of "conception trauma" ["*Trauma der Zeugung*"] (p. 40), which, as we saw, had already been postulated by various writers, such as Marie Bonaparte (1938), Fodor (1951), and Lietaert-Peerbolte (1952).

Lake (1973) has helped to increase our knowledge of the sort of images, metaphors, turns of phrase, and so on, that constitute the "language" of prenatality and may thus have made it possible to detect when a patient was unwittingly communicating something about how his experience of birth may have influenced his postnatal thinking and general behaviour.

Herbert Rosenfeld (1971), like Bion, has given us detailed descriptions of "parasitical" forms of transference in which the patient phantasies himself as living inside the analyst, but whereas Bion had described the more actively destructive aspects of such transferences, Rosenfeld showed how they can also take the form of a "sluggish and silent" sort of passivity (p. 117). He also later drew attention to the possibly intra-uterine nature of the phantasy of living inside the analyst (1983, p. 263) and hence also, by implication, to the prenatal nature of the parasitical forms of transference described by Bion and himself. Both these authors could, therefore, be said to have come very near to describing prenatal, object-seeking, and parasitical forms of transference in which aggressivity would play a considerable part. Rosenfeld's belief in the possible effect of prenatal influences was to become more explicitly stated in his last work (1987).

Anzieu (1974, p. 91) made an interesting observation about the fact that, as pointed out by Freud, "the ego of each individual member of a homogeneous group" tends to lose its autonomy and to submit to the authority of a group "ego". Referring to his concept of the "skin-ego" (1989) or "*Le moi-peau*" (1985), Anzieu further suggested that in large groups—where this loss of autonomy is even more marked than in small groups—the "skin-ego" of each individual member not only becomes merged with that of the large group but also, and in what I understand to be some kind of group regression at prenatal level, comes to be associated in the unconscious of each group member with the "skin" or inner lining of the inside of the prenatal mother's body (1974, p. 91). Anzieu's thoughts on autism (1985, pp. 230–231) also clearly show the importance he attached to the apparent need of autistic children to prolong the illusory feeling of still living inside the womb.

Foulkes, too, writing about the dynamic processes at work in group analysis (1971), had observed that in the transference the group could be unconsciously experienced by individual members, not only as the mother but also as the maternal womb. Ammon himself, who quotes both Anzieu and Foulkes, has not only written about what he calls the "uterine function" of the group, but has also shown how interpretations offered at prenatal level can sometimes help in group work (1974). He mentions the interesting example of a dream reported by one of the members of a therapeutic group in what was to be the last group session, and which the other members of the group immediately recognized as an unwitting description, by the dreamer, of how she had phantasied and experienced the disbanding of the group as a pregnant mother about to give birth to all her children (pp. 48–49). Like Graber, Ammon rejects the death instinct theory, which he finds "speculative" and "pessimistic" (1974, p. 58), but he is more specific than Graber in allowing for the possibility that a prenatal "unconscious ego-nucleus" ["*unbewusste Ich-Kern*"] may be damaged as early as *in utero* by prenatal trauma (p. 64), with the result that even the womb would then no longer be remembered by the patient's unconscious as a safe place to be in. I suspect with Ammon that this could then perhaps indeed become the background for certain permanent tension states in postnatal life (p. 64).

Burger-Piaget (1973) described how she had been able to offer significant help to three difficult prenatally regressed patients by means of interpretations offered at prenatal level and within the transference, and also how her countertransference had been affected by the patients' anxious, foetal demands for uninterrupted contact with her.

Laing himself (1976) wrote about prenatal life and its possible relevance to postnatal psychology. Most of his ideas, as he acknowledged in a footnote (p. 59), were taken from Mott. A seemingly valid question raised by Laing was that of what could be the effect on the psyche of losing, at birth, that part of our prenatal self which had been our main means of communication and exchange with our maternal environment: namely, the placental part of this erstwhile prenatal self (p. 58).

Grotstein (1978) could I think be said to have given us almost explicit descriptions of the overlap of foetal mechanisms into early postnatal forms of transference. He not only mentions the "diabolical parasitism" that characterizes certain forms of transference (p. 144), but he also wrote (p. 139) about patients in whom one can detect the postnatal persistence of a sense of "primary identificatory oneness" and who may "require interpretations which acknowledge their unbornness and their difficulty and/or reluctance in finding their way to a metaphoric 'birth canal'" (p. 146). In another work (1983b, p. 496), Grotstein wrote about the "background object of primary identification" as being "most closely associated with the womb-mother". I shall mention in chapter five some other aspects of Grotstein's work that could, I think, be said to have a bearing on the prenatal condition, although in a less explicit sort of way.

Sidney Klein, too, like Bion and Rosenfeld before him, has described transferences in which the patient phantasies himself as living inside the analyst. He has also made a significant observation: when writing about the "adhesive" quality of relatedness with which certain patients clung to him and about their phantasies of "being unborn" and of "living inside" him, he said that what these patients appeared to be looking for in him was a "placenta-like object which both feeds and detoxicates at the same time" (1980, p. 400). In a later work (1984), he similarly referred to another patient whose search for the ideal mother seemed to take the form of a search for a "placental object which fitted him perfectly at all points" (p. 313).

The patient whose therapy I report in chapter two, and to whom I had already alluded in an earlier work (Ployé, 1977, p. 144), also seems to me to have unconsciously wanted me to play the role of some placental mediator and communicating agent between herself and the hospital community in which she was being treated, and which she seemed to have unconsciously expected to function for her as the inside of the pregnant mother's body. Although Sidney Klein's main purpose in his 1980 paper was to illustrate how even well-adjusted patients can sometimes reveal the presence of autistic, "impenetrable", and "encapsulated" areas of their personality, his very well presented and interesting report could, I think, also be said to have shown, not only his awareness of the frequently prenatal nature of the patient's associations, but also his readiness to interpret some of these on prenatal lines and within the transference. The patient who had phantasied Klein's "inside" as that of a mother "full of riches" (p. 8), but who had also been afraid of venturing into this "inside" lest she became "buried alive" in it as in some collapsing mine-shaft (p. 8), also seems to me to have illustrated the "good womb/bad womb" type of dichotomy that Melanie Klein had thought might eventually be shown to antedate and "foreshadow" the good breast/bad breast type of split.

Mancia (1981, p. 353) has mentioned with apparent approval A. Rascovsky's notion of a "foetal ego" (1956), and he agreed with the idea that the death instinct should perhaps be conceived as operating as early as *in utero*—a suggestion that is not only to be found in the abovementioned 1956 paper by A. Rascovsky, as I pointed out earlier, but had, as we saw, already been put forward by Menninger as far back as 1939. Mancia also refers to foetal dreaming and to the modern research on the dreaming activity of "premature infants of six to seven months" (p. 352). In addition, he, too, is clearly interested in the possible existence, in the foetus, of what A. Rascovsky (1956, p. 288) has postulated as "proto-phantasies of phylogenetic origin", the latter being referred to by Mancia as "internal objects or inherited representations, independent of any experience with external objects" (p. 353).

Such "inherited representations" are clearly regarded by Mancia as preceding—and therefore as needing to be distinguished from—the "not-self" "things" that Bion thought the foetus might be able to vaguely sense as taking place around itself as a result of "happenings" or "events" such as those referred to earlier. If I have understood Mancia correctly, he conceives the foetus's experience of its maternal environment as building itself around, as well as being constantly "transformed" by, this nucleus of inherited predispositions, thus constituting what he calls "the beginning of a protomental activity in evolution" (p. 355); but, as Mancia also rightly points out, such "activity" would then present "some analogies with what Bion (1962) calls 'preconceptions'". He also attaches great importance, again rightly in my opinion, to what Bick (1968) and, later, Meltzer (1975) have had to say about the role played in the newborn by the skin, and he extends these speculations to the role that the skin could be deemed to play in the foetus's own experience. (See again in this connection the importance attached by Mott, 1964, pp. 43–58, 353–366, to the role of the "foetal skin" and also Anzieu's 1985, 1989, concept of the "skin-ego").

Verny (1981) has offered a wealth of examples of foetal reactivity and conditioning, and of the different ways in which prenatal events can shape and determine postnatal behaviour and experience. His report of what he believes to have been a case of foetal "temper" (p. 83) makes me think that he too probably agrees with the view that aggressivity is not something that occurs and expresses itself only after and as a result of birth. Could this be repeated in certain postnatal, angry, "knee-jerk" type of reactions?

Tustin (1981, p. 263, 1983, p. 183) has done much to extend Mahler's observations about the overlap of foetal modes of functioning and relating them to early postnatal life, and about how important it is for the infant not to be made to emerge too soon—or, for that matter, too late—from this extended postnatal and psychological "womb" in what is described as a second, psychological "birth". Tustin made a distinction, however, between this normal overlap in early infancy of some aspects of the foetal state and the truly "autistic"—that is, pathological—types of disorder, which show none of the "alertness and active questing" normally observed in early infancy (1991, p. 585).

The writings of the psycho-historian DeMause, although primarily concerned with the way in which the unresolved postnatal as well as prenatal psychopathology of individuals and groups—and, indeed, nations—can be acted out on a national or international scale, make very useful reading for anyone whose work normally revolves within the narrower confines of individual or group psychotherapy. DeMause himself makes several references to the possible existence of placental symbolism (1982, pp. 259–299). (Further mention of such possible symbols is made in chapter four.)[10]

Joseph (1983), like Bion, Rosenfeld, and others, has rightly emphasized the oral mechanisms involved in certain very primitive levels of transference, but her description (p. 100) of a patient whose "problem of being outside and born [had] never been adequately worked through", as well as what she says about patients who "do not 'act out' or miss the analyst in the holidays because they seem able to maintain [an] euphoric idealized relationship, living in a kind of continual presence which does not permit of any distance" (p. 95), seems to me not unlike the state of illusory "self-sufficiency" that Modell described as characteristic of the "cocoon" type of transference (1984, p. 98); and, as Modell pointed out in an earlier 1976 version of the chapter just quoted, this idealized relationship could be the acting out of a "womb phantasy" (p. 295). Despite her reference to the absence of any obvious acting out, Joseph, too, could therefore be said to have pointed to the silent and invisible acting out of a foetal or prenatal type of transference (see below and chapter five for further references to Modell and Joseph).

Grunberger (1983) has written about an "archaic", foetal "aggressivity" that has the body of the mother as object (pp. 925–926), and he, too, believes in the possibility of interpreting this aggressivity within the transference (p. 935). (See chapter five for a further reference to Grunberger's 1983 paper.)

Paul (1983), when referring to the Kleinian description of the infant's phantasied oral, anal, and urethral attacks on the mother's body, wrote (p. 563) that "attempts to forcefully gain nutrients and locate waste in the maternal object" may "not only relate to oral and anal aggressive phantasies", but also to "the attempt to maintain a functioning placenta as an expectation which has never been worked through".

I mention in chapter five Paul's description of a patient who not only felt "trapped" inside him but also gave rise in him to violent desires and impulses "to get rid of her in any way possible" (p. 559). The patient herself had experienced Paul as a threat to her security, and his office as a dangerous place where she might be trapped, damaged, mutilated, and so on. Repeated interpretations of the possibility of a severe birth trauma had seemed to help, and the patient had subsequently learnt that the mother, who had developed secondary uterine inertia when giving birth to her, had had to be delivered by Caesarean section.[11] Paul is also clearly interested, as Bion was, in the possibility of linking the mechanism of projective identification with the phantasy of being inside the mother's body (pp. 556–557) and his reference to the "attempt to maintain a functioning placenta" within that body makes me wonder whether he, too—as I was to do myself when writing the aforementioned 1984 paper on some aspects of Kleinian theory— had been thinking of the possible role played in such "projection" by the placenta. As in the case of Bion's *Bion in New York and São Paulo*, I much regret not having known of Paul's 1983 article when writing my own 1984 paper. What seems even more relevant to the particular theme of this book is Paul's belief that it is not only possible, but also useful and even necessary, to interpret certain types of material on prenatal lines and within the transference. (For a similar belief, see also below my reference to Share, 1994. Other references to Paul's work are made in chapter five.)

Lawson (1984), in an interesting piece of research, has uncovered vivid pre- and perinatal imagery in reports of UFO abduction by extraterrestrials. He also sees in such reports several instances of placental imagery. His main conclusion—which will, I imagine, be hotly contested by several of the people who have made these reports—is that such "experiences" are the intense reliving, out of the blue so to speak, of a prenatal or birth experience.

Modell (1984) has, as I said earlier, used the term "cocoon transference" (pp. 93–95) to describe a state of "non-relatedness" and illusory "self-sufficiency" that in his experience characterizes the transference during the first year or so of an analysis (p. 94), this self-sufficiency being a defence against what is really "a feared total dependence upon the human environment" (p. 94). He had previously pointed out (1976, p. 295) that such cocoon transferences "may be variations of a womb phantasy—a state where one is cut off from interaction from the environment, where one is not 'really in the world'", where there is "an illusion of self-sufficiency and yet a total dependence upon the care-taking functions of the maternal environment". I stand to be corrected on this, but I get the impression that the "insatiable" yearnings that Modell describes as beginning to break through with the gradual resolution of the cocoon transference are not intended by him to be understood as unresolved prenatal yearnings but, rather, as unresolved postnatal ones that had been concealed until then by the illusory "self-sufficiency"; and that the state of true relatedness that then follows can therefore be compared to the kind of relatedness with the mother into which the baby enters after its emergence from the womb. One of my reasons for saying this is that, in describing the release of the "insatiable" yearnings during the "dissolution" of the cocoon transference, Modell used the word "hatching" (1984, p. 98), which seems to me to evoke birth and hence the move to a postnatal kind of relatedness. When he wrote (on p. 295 of the early 1976 version) that in the cocoon the patient is "cut off from interaction from the environment" and is not "really in the world", I therefore understand Modell to have been referring to the postnatal "environment" or "world". My own proposal would be that the analyst can sometimes be used as the "cocoon", and that if the latter represents the womb or the prenatal mother, one then has to postulate a high degree of "interaction" or "relatedness" between the patient—in the role of the unborn child—and his maternal "environment"—represented now by the analyst.

Blomfield (1985) saw the placenta as that part of the foetus by means of which the latter parasitically attacks the mother's body. He quoted the concept of "placental parasitism" put forward in 1913 by the zoologist Giard,[12] and he, too (Blomfield, 1987, p. 309) regarded "projective identification" as the possible continuation, in postnatal mental life and in mental form, of the way in which the foetus "projects" its wastes via the placenta into the mother's bloodstream and then "identifies" with the mother by "introjecting" from her what it needs. In the second (1987) of the works referred to, entitled "Human Destructiveness: An Essay on Instinct, Foetal Existence and Infancy", Blomfield made it clear that he saw the prenatal stage as providing the "matrix" from which the subsequent stages of development are formed (p. 24). Moreover, he saw foetal parasitism as one of the roots of all human destructiveness (personal communication).

Maizels (1985) has suggested that certain dreams that appear to be birth dreams could, rather, point to a wish to *return* to the womb (emphasis added). As a possible example of this he mentioned a dream that Freud had interpreted as a birth dream, but without allowing for the possibility, in Maizels's opinion, that it might have signalled a "wish to dive *into* the womb" (emphasis in original) and, in the transference, Freud's "womb" (p. 186). This passage alone seems to me to imply some belief on Maizels's part in the possible existence of levels of transference that not only operate, but can also be interpreted, at prenatal level. A prenatal theme can, moreover, be said to pervade the whole of Maizels's paper. In his "reappraisal of the death instinct" (the subtitle of his paper and an important part of his thesis, as I understand it), he sees the threat posed to the ego by the death instinct as being closely associated—and almost interchangeable with—the threat posed to the "growing" and "active" ego by the wish to surrender to the "(parasitic) sleep-passivity tendency" to return to the womb (p. 191).

Alessandra Piontelli (1987, 1988, 1992) has carried out some remarkable research, through the use of ultrasound, into the possibility of "detecting early markers of character already *in utero*" (1987, p. 462). She has also described her analysis of a 2½-year-old girl who had tried to relive "her past life in the womb" in an apparent attempt to "protect" herself, by the "seemingly endless sensuous pleasure" this gave her, from "very strong feelings of jealousy of a very primitive kind" as well as from "having to re-experience her traumatic birth" (1988, p. 80). Piontelli's research seems to me to have not only demonstrated beyond doubt the relevance of prenatal life to postnatal mental life and behaviour, but also to have given us some idea of the therapeutic potential of whatever further investigations may be carried out regarding the possible prenatal determinants of postnatal behaviour.

As far as prenatal research itself is concerned, another important advance has been made by Piontelli's recent research on twins. Her 2002 book on twins has once again shown the importance of gathering facts. Among several of her findings, she has shown the differences that really exist in the physiology, intra-uterine behaviour, and environment of so-called "identical" (monozygotic) twins[13]—differences that will go on manifesting themselves in postnatal life (pp. 166–173). This has done much to dispel the frequently held belief in the "identical" nature of monozygotic twins and to establish their uniqueness; and it has made me recall the case of a very intelligent young man who was the senior member of a monozygotic twin couple, and whom I once had in therapy. It would be too long, as well as inappropriate, to quote his material in any great detail, but I had been struck by the fact that in the transference I seemed to represent this twin and that although my patient clearly seemed to experience me as closely linked to him by bonds of common sympathy and interest, there were also signs that I, as this younger twin, had to be carefully kept in check as some kind of rival in case I took a little more of the analytic "cake"—the blood of a commonly shared placenta?—than would have been good for the continued and well-ordered harmony of our relationship. Interpretations could go so far but no further. Piontelli's previous research had already shown that it could act as a powerful stimulus for psychoanalytic prenatal research; her 2002 book has likewise shown how it can provide an invaluable guide in checking the accuracy of our analytic interpretations and in helping us to understand the interaction between the patient and ourselves.

Dowling (1988, p. 535) has written a short but most interesting article on the "tree" as a possible placental symbol, and about the diagnostic and therapeutic possibilities provided by the use of this symbolism in directed dreams or phantasies.

Joan Symington's analysis of a mentally handicapped youth (1988) describes how he felt trapped inside her, as in the "web" of a womb-like "spider–mother" (p. 247). In his 1985 paper, Maizels had also referred to the spider symbolism to illustrate his thesis about the connection between the death instinct and the fear (as well as the wish) to return to the womb; and, as Maizels pointed out (on p. 191 of his own 1985 paper), Ogden had described a patient for whom spiders seemed to represent the "alluring and yet threatening" mother "of late symbiosis" who threatened to "haunt and suffuse the patient (or to be suffused by him) to the point that the two dissolve into one another—thus annihilating the patient as a separate entity" (Ogden, 1982, p. 196). Joan Symington's paper, from which her reference to the "spider mother" made me digress a little, thus seems to me to show that she, too, believes in not only the possibility, but also the usefulness, and even necessity of interpreting certain types of material on prenatal lines and within the transference.[14]

A paper by Hepper (1989) on foetal conditioning and "learning" offers a well-informed and comprehensive review of work on the subject up to 1989.

Chasseguet-Smirgel (1990) sees the postnatal type of aggressivity described by Melanie Klein and others—an aggressivity that consists in wanting to force a way into the mother's body to scoop out or befoul its contents, and so on—as having as its primary goal that of rediscovering and re-experiencing "a universe without obstacles, without roughness or differences, identified with the mother's abdomen". Her proposal, based on clinical material, is that behind the wish to destroy or appropriate the phantasized contents of the mother's inside—father's penis, babies, faeces, and so on—"a more basic archaic wish can be detected": that of returning to the "smooth" inside of the mother's womb after all the above "obstacles" have been removed from it. (More detailed references to Chasseguet-Smirgel's work, and to what she has to say about the possible prenatal roots of the Oedipus complex and the prenatal phase generally (1990, 1992), are made below.)

Whyte (1991) has shown his awareness of how the "foetal-maternal placental junction" that exists in prenatal life, as well as the physical and chemical exchanges that take place in it between mother and foetus, could be the prototypes and precursors of all object relations and also of the psychological mechanisms of projection, introjection, and identification. He quotes several of the authors to whom I have referred here and appears to think that Ogden's concept of an "autistic-contiguous position" can be regarded as having strong connotations of what I suggest one could call the prenatal "position"—a view to which I return in chapter five.

Although complimentary about its clinical material, Rowan (1991, pp. 206–207) has criticized Whyte's paper on the grounds that it not only rejects too easily the possibility of any consciousness in the unborn child, or of any—in Whyte's words—"mental functioning complex enough to be called psychological life", but it also describes the uterine condition as approaching "the ideal" since the foetus—again in Whyte's words—is "not aware of any frustration or deprivation". Rowan is very aware of the usefulness of conceiving of a "good womb/bad womb" dichotomy, and since he does not quote Melanie Klein's own idea on the subject (1957, p. 492), he must have arrived at it independently. He has also pushed it even further by pointing out that "bad womb experiences are even worse than bad breast experiences because the chance of any real escape is not there" (p. 207). These words from Rowan could be said to sum up neatly much of what I have been trying to say in this book. Concerning the question of whether the foetus could be deemed to have any consciousness, it is difficult to deny it at least a degree of consciousness when one reads the work of Piontelli, and also the following vivid and amusing description, by DeMause, of the foetus in action (1982, p. 253):

> The foetus during the second trimester, while the amniotic sack is still rather roomy, now floats peacefully, now kicks vigorously, turns somersaults, hiccoughs, sighs, urinates, swallows and breathes amniotic fluid and urine, sucks its thumbs, fingers and toes, grabs its umbilicus, gets excited at sudden noises, calms down when the mother talks quietly, and gets rocked back to sleep as she walks about.

Naomi Rucker (1994) has written an excellent paper, based on clinical material, on how the "intense, and often unconscious, affect exchange between analyst and patient, which often remains an intangible undercurrent in the analytic process, harks back to the process that connects mother and foetus" (p. 219). One of Paul's papers (1989) is quoted in the reference section of Rucker's paper under the title: "Notes on the primordial development of the perinatal transference". The words "perinatal transference" intrigued me, since they seemed to be describing the kind of transference I shall suggest could perhaps be deemed to have obtained in the way that my Patient A had managed to get herself "born out of" me at the end of the therapy. I therefore wrote to Dr Paul, who very kindly sent me a copy of his 1989 paper, and I saw that in Rucker's list of references on page 220 of her own paper and in the 1989 reference to Paul, the words "the perinatal transference" should have been "the penitential transference". This amusing error must presumably have been due to the fact that the main theme of Paul's paper had been that patients who appear to feel imprisoned within a particularly severe, punitive, and hence *"penitential"* form of superego can sometimes be deemed or even be known to have suffered from particularly severe forms of *perinatal* trauma (see the summary of Paul's 1989 paper, pp. 43, 48), and I found myself thinking again here about how in addition to springing from strong feelings of guilt, Patient A's feeling of being "in some kind of self-imposed prison" had also appeared to have had strong connotations of feeling trapped and closed in within the suffocating and persecutory inside of a mother in labour (second admission, Session 16, and others).[15]

Also in 1994, Share described how birth and even prenatal trauma can sometimes be reconstructed by means of dreams and other symbolic material, and how this, as also suggested by Rucker, can sometimes have good therapeutic results. Like Paul, whose 1983 paper I mentioned earlier, Share makes clear her belief not only in the possibility, but also in the usefulness and even necessity of interpreting certain types of material on prenatal lines and within the transference. She also shows how certain patients can be seen to unconsciously act out, in their relatedness to the therapist, what can later be confirmed as having been such prenatal or birth trauma, and how the therapist, too, can be made to experience or even be in danger of acting out, in his or her countertransference, some of the more traumatic—and traumatizing—aspects of the reactions that the patient's mother herself had gone through during pregnancy and/or confinement. This is shown in particular in Share's clinical example No. 1 (p. 185), which does appear to suggest, as she herself points out, that if she had not been able to "hold" and "contain" the patient by her understanding the latter's birth experience, she (Share) would perhaps have been a little like the patient's mother whose "incompetent cervix" (p. 190) had made it necessary to resort to a birth by Caesarean section.[16] The whole of her book, which incidentally provides extremely useful information about the biological, obstetrical, and physiological side of prenatal research, also makes it clear that Share believes, like Paul and as I do myself, that much of what is often described as womb "phantasies" may in fact be nothing less than unconscious "memories" that can be uncovered in sessions by means of dreams, other symbolic material, or even patterns of behaviour past or present, including the patient's "here-and-now" experience of the sessions themselves.

This last point was also made by Rucker in her own 1994 paper, and indeed by many of the writers who have given any thought to the persistence in postnatal life of prenatal modes of experience and reactivity.

Before the publication of Share's book, both she (1992) and another member of the Los Angeles group, Dr Erna Osterweil (1990), had each written a doctoral dissertation on a prenatal subject. I draw this to the attention of eventual readers because both of these dissertations also contain a mine of useful information about the biological as well as the psychological side of prenatal research.

J. Mitrani (1996, pp. 151–203) has described what she calls "adhesive pseudo-object" forms of relationship, which, she believes, could be "rooted in traumatic experiences of extreme deprivation occurring *in utero* (emphasis in original) and/or in early infancy" (1996, p. 150). (More is be said about this in chapter five.)

Working with autistic children, and strongly indebted, as is Mitrani, to the pioneering work of Tustin, Maiello has provided further evidence in support of the latter's belief that autistic disorders may have their origin in prenatal trauma (1997, p. 9, 2001). (I return to Maiello's work—for example, 1995, 1997, 2001— below.)

Wilheim, whom I have mentioned already, has been carrying out some interesting research on whether the interaction that takes place at cellular and biochemical level between the germ cells during their mating, and the continuation of this interaction in the growing individual, could be thought to lay the foundations of some kind of proto-mind that then impresses its stamp on all later stages of development. If I understand Wilheim correctly, her proposal seems to be that even when a patient's feeling of internal conflict can fairly convincingly be attributed to the continuing quarrel within himself of parents who had in fact quarrelled with each other when he was a child, it might be worth asking oneself whether such a child—and now patient—had been made more vulnerable to such quarrels by some kind of "conception shock" in which the cellular "mating" of his father's sperm and mother's ovum had already in some way been conflictual. As we have seen, the hypothesis of "conception shock" had already been put forward by various writers, such as Marie Bonaparte (1938), Fodor (1949) and Lietaert-Peerbolte (1975, pp. 24–41, 134–144, 185, 293–294), but Wilheim (1988) believes that it could be extended much further than has been done by these earlier writers. When writing to me in 1993, she told me that she had been collecting abundant and detailed clinical material over the previous years. If this material has been published and can convincingly demonstrate the clinical applicability and therapeutic usefulness of Wilheim's hypothesis in the day-to-day work with patients, this could well constitute an important step towards our understanding of "the mind" and how it works—or doesn't work.

Riccardo Steiner's own awareness of the importance of prenatal trauma on later development is clearly shown in his 1999 paper about a young painter (see p. 700 in particular): but more important still, it seems to me, is the way it also shows Steiner's belief in the possibility—indeed the usefulness—of interpreting the patient's relatedness to the analyst on prenatal lines when appropriate. (See, for example, on p. 699, Steiner's interpretation of his patient's dream about a little frog that had come to experience the "pond" and amniotic waters of Steiner's womb as no longer dangerous.)

Some of the writers mentioned so far—for example, Sidney Klein (1980, p. 400, 1984, p. 313), and Paul (1983, p. 561)—have referred to the placenta as the main "object" of foetal libido and aggressivity, whereas Grunberger (1983, pp. 925–926) has, as we saw, described foetal "aggressivity" as having as its object the body of the prenatal mother. Since Blomfield (1985, 1987) appears to see the placenta as the part of the foetus that parasitically attacks the host—namely, here again, the prenatal mother—he, too, presumably regarded, like Grunberger, the main object of foetal aggressivity as being the mother herself. The material I present in chapter two seems to me to suggest that my patient sometimes perceived and treated me as if I were a "prenatal mother" type of object, at other times as a "placental" object, and sometimes as both simultaneously.

The above survey of some of the writings that have already either touched on or been devoted to the possible existence and interpretability of prenatal transferences, as well as to the possible usefulness of conceiving of a prenatal form of aggressivity, has probably been far too long already without being complete. It would be remiss of me, however, if I did not also mention the important contributions to the subject by writers such as Blarer (1973), Caruso (1973), Eichenberger (1973), W. E. Freud (1985, 1988a, 1988b, 1989), Grof (1976, 1983), Haesler (1974), Hau (1973; Hau & Schindler, 1982), Janus (1986, 1988, 1990), Kruse (1969, 1973a, 1973b), Laibow (1988), Sarkissoff (1974), Schindler (1973, 1975, 1982a, 1982b, 1988),

Schusser (1988), Van den Bergh (1988), and others. The number of publications on the subject has increased so rapidly in recent years that it is difficult to keep up with them.

Finally, and although publications only concerned with observations of foetal behaviour cannot be expected to deal with the day-to-day preoccupations of psychoanalytic or psychotherapeutic work in the consulting-room, they, too, should be mentioned here, not only because of their interest and their relevance to psychiatry generally, but because a better knowledge of prenatal development and foetal behaviour—dare one say psychology?—should presumably help us to know what to look for in our attempts to help patients, just as observational studies of infants' behaviour have done in the past and are likely to go on doing for some time. Some of the publications I have particularly in mind here are those of Gesell (1945), Hepper (1989), Hooker (1952, 1964), Joffe (1969), Liley (1967, 1972), Montagu (1964), and Sontag (1940, 1941, 1944, 1966),[17] to quote but a few. (For an overall review of the biological work done in this field, see also Osterweil, 1990, and Share, 1992.)

Returning now to the question of whether the possible effectiveness of interpreting presumed prenatal material within the transference could be enhanced by making use of the hypothesis of prenatal aggressivity, it is interesting to note that although, as far as I can see, none of the various writers who have favoured this view appear to have been guided by considerations derived from biology, those who have studied the relatedness between the embryo and the mother's body from the physical point of view have in fact described it as involving an aggression of the latter by the former. The words "prenatal aggressivity" do not figure in the two passages I am about to quote, but I think they can be said to be strongly implied. Both quotations relate to the interaction that takes place between the newly fertilized egg and the uterine wall six or seven days after conception: more precisely, between the *trophoblast* (that part of the egg's periphery whose function it is to eat its way into the uterine wall and enable the egg to get "embedded" there), and the *endometrium* (the lining of uterine cells on that wall into which the "embedding" will take place).

The first quotation is from Hamilton, Boyd, and Mossman (1945, p. 53):

The trophoblast apparently possesses the power of destroying and ingesting endometrial cells which thus constitute a "pabulum" for the growing embryo before the establishment of a functional placenta. The embryo–mother relationship is biologically very similar to a parasite–host relationship with, normally, a perfect balance between the invasive activity of the trophoblast (parasite) on the one hand and the protective reaction of the endometrium (host) on the other. In some cases, however, the relationship may become disturbed in either direction. Pathological overactivity of the trophoblast results in the formation of a hydatiform mole or a chorioepithelioma. If the endometrium is too resistant, the result will be death with absorption or abortion of the foetus.

The second quotation is from Rushton:

The trophoblast... is a naturally invasive tissue and during implantation penetrates the endometrial surface. The adjacent cells undergo necrosis, the debris being phagocytosed by the syncytial cells... the endometrial vessels are eroded.

Rushton then goes on to point out that the uterine environment "plays a major part in preventing uncontrolled trophoblastic invasion" and that in animals "extra-uterine blastocysts—for example, blastocysts implanted in the brain or testis—show uncontrolled trophoblastic proliferation, which destroys these organs" (1973, p. 345).

Such biological data do therefore seem to me to go some way towards supporting the feasibility and possible usefulness of a hypothesis according to which the fertilized egg, the embryo, and the foetus would all possess a primary, basic, but healthy kind of aggressivity that, when adequately met by the mother's body, would remain within normal bounds and lead to healthy growth but that would, depending on whether the mother's endometrium had proved too resistant or too compliant, either turn upon itself and end in death by miscarriage or go the other way and become the uncontrolled, pathological aggressivity referred to in the quotations above. If we wished to apply this to our everyday psychoanalytic work and to a further study of the interactional–adaptational processes so well described by Langs (1976, Vol. 2, pp. 311–329), could a patient sometimes be said to react to a rigid, overdefended, and insufficiently empathetic countertransference as if it were the psychological equivalent of what Hamilton described as an over-resistant endometrium—a kind of resistance that, in the case of a patient whose hold on life was not too vigorous, could then lead to his attempting or committing suicide? And if an insufficiently firm response to the patient's unrealistic demands led to equally bad results by allowing him too much invasiveness, could this conversely be said to repeat a past situation in which not only the parents or the early postnatal mother, but also the prenatal mother herself, had not been able to keep his aggressivity under sufficient control? One could also evoke here Winnicott's idea that patients can only begin to properly trust and hence "use" the therapy when the latter has not only enabled them to release on the analyst the full extent of their destructiveness, but also shown them that both the work and the analyst's person have "survived" this destructiveness.

Finally, should anyone require some help in imagining how the "language" of biology could be fused with that of psychology—at least where prenatal life is concerned—I cannot think of anything better than to quote a 2001 article by Donald Meltzer and Meg Harris Williams. I particularly liked Meltzer's reference to the placenta (p. 36), but what I thought was even more remarkable was his ability to identify himself, and in such a human way, with what could well be the "experience" of the unborn child.[18] In an earlier (1988) joint publication by Meltzer and Harris Williams, Meltzer too, like DeMause, had incidentally shown his awareness of the fact that birth could well be sometimes experienced as a welcome "escape' from a not particularly pleasant prenatal world, and not simply as an expulsion from some kind of Paradise (pp. 17, 21).[18]

NOTES

1. I regret that this "Review" is almost certainly not as up-to-date as I would have liked it to be.

2. For the history of the foundation and development of the original ISPP, see Graber, 1972, pp. 6–8, 1973, pp. 19–20; for its evolution and development after Graber, see Fedor-Freybergh and Vogel, 1988, p. XIX and particularly pp. 607–618.

3. Alice Balint (1939), when writing about "primary object-love" herself, preferred the term "primary" or "archaic"—rather than "passive"—to describe

this early type of "love" or "object-relation" (p. 127). The term "passive" did not seem to her to do justice to its intensely "active" and "clinging" component—a point I shall return to in connection with the notion of prenatal "aggressivity".

4. The words *"effraction du protoplasme"*, used in the French original version (*Revue Française de Psychanalyse*, 1936, 9: 422–429) was rendered in the 1938 English translation as "irruption into the protoplasm": *"effraction"* in French has strong connotations of "breaking and entering": *"vol avec effraction"*, for example, is the term for "burglary", as opposed to "theft" or "robbery".

5. Freud had said very much the same thing in 1920 in *Beyond the Pleasure Principle* (see, e.g., 1920g, pp. 40, 48, 50).

6. In her early writings Klein had held that destructive impulses—aggression—made their first appearance with the separation from the mother at birth and the resulting loss of intra-uterine security (1948, p. 278); and she had also seen the first few weeks of postnatal life as the starting point of all future object relationships (1946, p. 293)—a view that, notwithstanding her subsequent speculations about the conceivability of a good womb/bad womb kind of dichotomy, she seems to have held at least until 1952 (see p. 199 of her paper on "some theoretical conclusions regarding the emotional life of the infant", 1952b). I understand, however, that Osterweil has recently referred to the womb and the umbilical cord as being the "first object relationship" (*Journal of the American Psychoanalytic Association*, 2003, p. 677).

7. I regret not to have known about Bion's 1980 book in time to quote, in my 1984 paper on certain aspects of Kleinian theory, his own suggestion about the possible prenatal origin of the psychological process known as "projective identification". On the same subject, see also below my reference to what other writers, such as Blomfield (1985), Paul (1983), and Whyte (1991), have themselves said about the possible prenatal origins of "projective identification".

8. I presume Bion would have been aware of some of the publications that had already appeared on the subject of foetal reactivity and conditioning, some of which are listed below. On the other hand, he may well have been relying solely on what he calls "speculative imagination" (1980, p. 27).

9. The first of which, *Ambivalenz des Kindes*, 1924, was, as I said, published in the same year as Rank's book on the *Birth Trauma*; it has since then been reproduced, considerably enlarged, in the 1975 edition of his *Gesammelte Schriften* [Collected Papers] under the title, "Ursprung, Zwiespalt und Einheit der Seele").

10. for anyone interested in the subject of prenatal life and its relevance to postnatal psychology, the last chapter of DeMause's 1982 book *The Foundations of Psychohistory*—pp. 244–297 in particular—will prove extremely helpful.

11. Neville Symington (personal communication, 1987) has described to me a similar experience with a prenatally regressed patient who felt trapped inside him and caused him to experience countertransference reactions similar to the one described by Paul. In his remarkable paper on the psychotherapy of a subnormal patient, Symington wrote that he had sometimes come across what appeared to be a "foetal" type of "transference" in physically handicapped patients (1981, p. 195).

12. Giard's works were published posthumously in 1913, five years after his death in 1908.

13. Monozygotic twins: twins who result from the division in two of the fertilized egg or zygote and who, although they each have their own individual umbilical cord, are attached to only one placenta, whose blood they share.

14. Abraham (1922) had already pointed out that "spiders" could be used by the unconscious to symbolize phantasied and feared aspects of the mother—of her genitalia, in particular. The fear of getting and remaining entangled in a placental and maternal "web" would then presumably represent an even deeper fear?

15. See also Mason's (1983, p. 143) proposals concerning the possible usefulness of conceiving of a "surrounding", "suffocating", and "crushing" form of superego, and for my belief that the latter too could have its origins in the "surrounding" kind of "pressure" which Paul (1990, pp. 13, 15) again traces to the birth experience. Please note that all subsequent references to Mason's proposals about the possible existence of a "surrounding", "suffocating", and "crushing" kind of superego give 1983 as the date of the relevant paper. It was in fact first published in 1981 by Caesura Press, but the version I have been using here is the 1983 version reprinted by Karnac, and the pages referred to here are therefore those from this edition.

16. In addition to this example No. 1, and as further instances of Share's consummate skill at reconstructing pre- and perinatal trauma by means of dreams, see in particular her clinical examples No. 3 (p. 196), 5 (p. 207), and 7 (p. 216).

17. As mentioned earlier, a more complete list of such publications, at least up to 1989, has been given by Hepper (1989).

18. My thanks are due to Neville Symington for having drawn my attention to that most interesting article.

19. I am also indebted to Neville Symington for having drawn my attention to a book by Pierce Clark which was published and dedicated to Freud in the same year (1933) as the latter's *New Introductory Lectures*. This book was entitled: *The Nature and Treatment of Amentia* and was a study of mental handicap. It gives striking examples of how such patients still crave and search for the sensation of once again being engulfed and held within the safe body of the mother they had lost at birth (pp. 27, 50, 58, 62, and others).

CHAPTER TWO

Clinical material

PATIENT A

Patient A was a young woman who, several years ago, and between the ages of 20 and 22, had two periods of inpatient therapy at the hospital where I used to work. Her first admission lasted only a fortnight; her second, about a year later, about 5½ months. I was her therapist on both occasions.

She had been referred to us by a psychiatric hospital near her home. The referral letter had told us that her father had declared himself unable or unwilling to finance the cost of her attending a university away from home. He and she had apparently been getting on very well together when she was a child, but in her teens he had switched his affections to her sister, who was older than she by about 18 months. She had begun to "stand up" to him, and bitter quarrels had ensued, culminating in the father's refusal to pay the cost of her attending a university away from home. She had had to content herself with a university nearby, had not been happy there, and had made a serious suicide attempt, which had led to her admission to the above-mentioned psychiatric hospital. The various forms of general psychiatric help that had been tried there had not been deemed successful, and the referral to us had been made in the hope that psychotherapy would produce better results.

The referral letter had also told us that Miss A's father tended to see himself as "the Commander-in-Chief of the whole family", that her mother was a cripple and tended to be treated by the rest of the family as a helpless and dependent child, and that Miss A was engaged to be married.

The transference
and what was deemed to be its prenatal underscoring

The first admission

Session 1

The first meeting between Patient A and me took place in my hospital office, on a Friday morning, following her arrival at the hospital the day before. I invited her to sit in the armchair opposite mine, and after she had confirmed that the information contained in the referral letter, which I read to her, was correct, I further invited her to tell me a little more about herself.

She straightaway told me that she felt that "everyone" had "got it in for (her) here" and that she had had that feeling from the moment she had crossed the hospital front door on arrival and a nurse had taken her around the place and introduced her to other patients. Almost without stopping, she then went on to say that her father had "destroyed (her) potential" by not making it possible for her to attend the university of her choice; that when she had had to be admitted to hospital for her psoriasis (her most distressing and painful condition), he had accused her of "sponging on the State" by "needing hospitals"; that her childhood had been ruined by the fact that she had been expected to act as nurse to her invalid mother and thus been prevented from playing with other children; that she was determined to die: she would eventually find a secluded spot where no one would find her, and kill herself. She then stopped and seemed to want some kind of response from me. All I could find to say was that, particularly in view of the very firm way in which she had just spoken of her determination to kill herself, she, too, seemed to have "got it in" for herself and to therefore be in danger of "destroying" whatever "potential" we might be able to help her salvage from what she felt had already been done to it by her father. She shook her head vigorously at this, and although she said nothing and her eyes were averted, it was clear that she disagreed completely with what I had just said myself: in other words, she had not "got it in" for herself and had no intention of destroying whatever we might be able to do for her. I missed seeing that this exchange could have been a muted repetition of the "quarrels" that had taken place between her and her father in her teens and in which she had begun to "stand up" to him.

The interview was drawing to its close, and I just had time to thank her and tell her that I would be seeing her from then on three times a week, on Mondays, Wednesdays, and Fridays, for 45 minutes each time.

Session 2

When she arrived for her next session on the Monday, I told Miss A that I would like our further talks to take place with her using the couch and myself sitting slightly behind her. She complied, but after saying that she felt a little "threatened" by the new situation, she got hold of the blanket and covered herself with it from head to foot, saying she felt "safer that way". Her sister, she went on, had sometimes "mothered" her, and this had helped. When she (Miss A) had mentioned this to the nurse who had been assigned to her, the nurse had apparently disagreed and said that "wasn't the way", but she was wrong. In any case, Miss A said, she had found out that this nurse was the same age as her sister, and this "might make things difficult". I said that in putting the blanket over herself she had probably arranged for a bit of self-mothering, but that her feeling "safer that way" suggested a need to protect herself from what might otherwise be experienced as an "unsafe" me: perhaps a father me, like the one she had started to quarrel with in her teens? Miss A countered this again by saying that she felt "safer" with me than "anywhere else in the hospital", and the session had again to end on that note.

Session 3

After covering herself up again with the blanket, Miss A started by saying that her "act" had "come back". This was the act of "acting cheerful" when she felt that people were getting too near her feelings of unhappiness, hate, or depression. The importance of this was to reveal itself later. At some point in that session, Miss A also gave me the first glimpse of what was later to reveal itself, particularly in the second admission a year or so later, as the extent and intensity of her unresolved foetal yearnings.

She said, for example, that the only way she could feel "really safe and completely (her)self" was to spin an imaginary cocoon around herself. She showed me what she meant by tracing an imaginary spiral in the air, starting at her head and ending towards her feet, and she added that it "would be damaging to break the cocoon". I said that the "cocoon" made me think of the womb; that she probably took refuge in one of these imaginary "wombs" when she felt that people had "got it in" for her, as she had felt to be the case almost from the moment of her coming through our hospital front door on admission; and that since she had said in the previous session that she felt "safer" with me than anywhere else in the hospital, being with me probably gave her a feeling of intrauterine security, away from a hospital community that, in addition to probably representing the unhappy home situation, may also be experienced by her as the harsher world of postnatal reality. Miss A agreed with this. I then went on to say that her warning that it might be "damaging" to "break the cocoon" could be construed as her telling me not to be a disapproving father who might "accuse" her of "sponging" on the security of the blanket and her sessions, and therefore want to break the "cocoon" to get her out of it, thus "damaging" the vulnerable and unborn part of herself that had sought refuge inside it. In keeping once again with what had already appeared to be her reluctance to associate me with anything bad, Miss A silently shook her head, thus indicating that she did not see me as a father who might begrudge her using me as a kind of womb or prenatal mother.

* * *

The reason for her first stay with us being so short was that on the 14th day, a Thursday, Patient A had made another suicide attempt, which could have been fatal and which aroused our anxieties to such an extent that in view of our limited facilities for containing patients with severe behaviour problems, we had deemed it no longer safe to continue with her treatment and had arranged for her return to the psychiatric hospital.

The sequence of events had been as follows. On the morning of that particular Thursday, Miss A's individually appointed nurse had approached me to ask me whether, in view of the fact that Miss A had apparently been "talking suicide" to some of her fellow patients the evening before, I wanted to see her for an extra session: as I had arranged to see her on Mondays, Wednesdays, and Fridays, Thursday was a non-session day. Misled by what had seemed to be Miss A's particularly cheerful and "jokey" mood in her Wednesday session the day before, I told the nurse that I thought things could wait until the next session on the Friday, but to let me or the duty doctor know if there was any cause for concern.

On returning to work on the Friday, I saw in the daily Nursing Report that just as lunch was about to be served on the Thursday, Miss A had approached her nurse and asked her if she could "have a word". The nurse had just promised to help another patient over lunch and had asked Miss A if it would be all right for her to do this first and see Miss A half an hour or so later. On Miss A's twice repeated assurance that she could wait, the nurse had gone to attend to the other patient. Barely ten minutes later Miss A had left the hospital and acted out what I later concluded must have been a mixture of rage and despair by putting her life at risk in a way that, I was given to understand, could have left her seriously or even fatally injured.

I was also told that the nurse had been very upset by this and that her colleagues were rallying round her in support, angry about the way that Miss A had misled her into thinking that she could wait. I suspected that Miss A's anger or despair had not been against the nurse alone for not seeing through her: that I myself must have failed to see or do something that Miss A had expected me to see or do in the Wednesday session and that, if so, this must then have caused the unfortunate nurse to get a double dose of Miss A's anger, namely that which Miss A had felt against the nurse for not attending to her on the spot but also that to which I thought I may have given rise in her myself in the Wednesday session 24 hours earlier, the precise reasons for which were still unknown to me. (I did later get some idea of what could have gone wrong, but to explain would be to digress.)

In order to have an up-to-date account to give of Miss A's state of mind before the daily Unit Staff meeting, I arranged to see her for her Friday session earlier than usual. She strenuously denied having been disappointed in me as a result of the Wednesday session, said she was very sorry for what she had done, and she hoped it would not bring about her discharge. (She had already become aware of the commotion that her acting out had caused among the nursing staff.)

At the Staff meeting it was clear that in addition to being angry and upset, the nurses of the Unit were concerned about the risk involved if they and the nurses of the other Units were expected to be responsible for such an unpredictable and impulsive patient during nights and weekends when there was only one nurse and one night orderly on the premises and the duty doctor was only on call at the end of a telephone. I told the meeting that Miss A had appeared to be repentant about what she had done and concerned about whether she would be allowed to stay, but that, apart from suspecting that I must have missed something in the Wednesday session, I still had no idea what this could have been; that I could not, therefore, make any prediction about how long it might take to help her to bring her impulsiveness a little more under control; and that as I, too, was concerned about the fact that the weekend would be starting within a few hours, I was prepared to get in touch with the referring hospital to see whether Miss A could be re-admitted there that same afternoon. This was accepted, and I left the meeting to make the necessary arrangements. The duty doctor at the other hospital said there would be no problem, and I sent for Miss A to tell her what was happening.

She appeared rather crestfallen and then started to tell me that when she was a child, her paternal grandparents had for some reason taken an intense dislike to her and reserved all their affection for her older sister. The latter had been "their life" and could do "no wrong" in their eyes; and although much "worse behaved", as a child, than Miss A felt she had been herself, this sister had always been able to "get away with murder" while Miss A herself "kept being told off for trifles". Her mother, Miss A continued, had been "supportive" but had not been able to do much more than show her that she was on her side, for example by trying to comfort her with such remarks as: "They [meaning the grandparents and hence the mothers-in-law] have never accepted us, you and me".

Miss A did not appear to have any conscious realization of what I felt to be the significance of what she had just been telling me, namely that she was perhaps seeing the nurses as disapproving grandparents who were blaming her for having upset their favourite grandchild, now represented by Miss A's personal nurse. (Later I was also to recall what Miss A had said in Session 2 about her nurse being the same age as her sister, and how this "might make things difficult".)

This glimpse into what at least some of us appeared to be acting out having made me a little more hopeful about the possibility of making sense of things after all, I told Miss A that what she had just said had given me an idea that I needed to discuss with the rest of the team; that I was therefore bringing the session to a close, and that I would be sending for her later. I then went to see the Senior Nurse of the Unit to ask her if in the light of "new material"—the nature of which I did not specify—she and her colleagues might be prepared to persevere a little longer. She was very angry; she said that she had already prepared the other patients of the Unit for Miss A's departure that afternoon, but she accepted my suggestion that we ask the Head of the Unit for advice. We both joined the latter in his office, but after careful deliberation my colleague thought that it would, on balance, probably be better if Miss A returned to the referring hospital as originally decided. I therefore sent for Miss A again to let her know. Her response was rather striking: "You are on trial for your life, they are denying me to you and they are also denying me the right to live my life as they live theirs." I wasn't too sure what to make of the second half of this remark, but the first part of it seemed to me to mean that she saw or wanted to see me as the "Daddy" whose favourite child she had been in earlier years, who would now be sad to lose his little girl and who would, if he defended her against the anger of his parents—represented here by the nursing "grandparents" and the rest of the team—have a hard time defending his own position as a member of the team "family".

I should perhaps mention here that throughout all this I made no mention to anyone, including Miss A herself, of what I had thought to be the significance of the material about the paternal grandparents. My fear had been that my mere mention of it would cause the nurses to think that I was blaming them for the way they were reacting to Miss A, and that the latter might also use the new understanding to see herself once again as being unjustly treated. In addition to this, I felt that there was a lot of unhappiness and aggressivity left in her that needed to be worked through before Miss A could make proper use of insights of that nature. All this, incidentally, happened years ago—long before the advances that inpatient psychotherapy has made in the course of the last few decades have resulted in nurses developing an interest in the various ways in which patients' unresolved past experiences can play a part in causing staff to react in this or that way towards them.

On the Monday following Miss A's departure, and as a result of having to write a discharge report, I found what it was that could have gone wrong in the Wednesday session. It would take too long to go over this here, except to say that my mishandling of that session appears to have affected the situation by contributing to the suicidal gesture that had set in motion the reactions of all of us.

When looking at things from a purely postnatal point of view, I thought that the ways we had all reacted to Miss A's suicidal gesture could perhaps be described as one in which the various roles had been distributed as follows:

1. The nurses seemed to me to have been given the role of disapproving grandparents who had been angry about the way that Miss A had upset her nurse, the latter having thus become the favourite granddaughter who could do no wrong.

2. I seemed to have reacted like a supportive but rather ineffectual mother who, by asking for a postponement of Miss A's discharge, had tried to counteract the hostility of the nursing staff/grandparents but whose wish had not been "accepted" by the team—any more than Miss A's mother had been "accepted" by her in-laws.

3. The head of the team seemed to have been put in the position of a "father" who had decided against risking the (emotional)

"cost" of enabling Miss A to continue with her sessions—somewhat in the same way, perhaps, as her real father had been unable or unwilling to meet the (financial) "cost" of enabling Miss A to attend a university away from home. Miss A had clearly felt happier with her sessions with me than with her life in the rest of a therapeutic community, where she felt that everyone "had it in" for her and which could, therefore, have represented the "unhappy home situation" from which she was not completely able to get away, even when with me in her sessions.

The second admission

Following her discharge from us and back at the psychiatric hospital, Miss A did not lose hope, and with the knowledge and approval of her consultant she wrote to us asking whether she could be given a second chance. Her first two letters, which were addressed to me and which I passed on to the Head of the Unit, did not cause the latter to change his mind, but a third letter, addressed to my colleague direct and appealing to him "on the grounds of humanity"—I think those were the words—did finally result in his agreeing to give Miss A this second chance, and with me again as her therapist.

Miss A's readmission was preceded by a letter from the psychiatric hospital saying she had become anorectic. We found this to be indeed the case, but I cannot recall asking myself whether this new development could be telling us something about her further appetite for psychotherapy, despite her obvious keenness to come back to us. In addition to the concern aroused in us by the anorexia itself, Miss A gave rise to another kind of anxiety and frustration by completely withdrawing from the nursing staff and her fellow-patients and speaking to no one except to me in sessions. This isolation from the hospital community caused several people to say that she seemed to be living "in a world of her own".

Thinking, perhaps wrongly, that the difficulties encountered by all of us in the first admission may have been contributed to, even indirectly, by the use of the couch, I told Miss A that she might as well use the chair from now on.

In *Session 3* of this second admission Miss A said that her not eating had caused the nursing staff to institute a special diet for her—mostly "baby food"—that she could eat under supervision and not reject later. I inquired about early feeding. All she knew was that she had been breast fed by her mother for about four months, that her sister had been at the breast for much longer than that, and that she (Miss A), had always seen this as "proof" that there had been "more love" for her sister than for her "right from the start".

When I was later to compare the two admissions and look upon them as a whole, it occurred to me that in the first admission, and when Miss A's nurse had explained to her that she could not attend to her straightaway because she had previously promised to help another patient over lunch, this other patient may have become unconsciously associated in Miss A's mind with a favoured sister whose oral needs had been considered more urgent than her own, and that this may have contributed to Miss A's impulsive and suicidal acting out a few minutes later.

Miss A also told me in this session that she had once locked herself up in a public lavatory and swallowed some tablets and some whisky in an attempt to kill herself. She had nearly died but had been found just in time. This was later to make me wonder whether she had been acting out an experience of "near death" *in utero*, in the "locked-up" conditions of the containing womb. (Joseph's own interest in experiences of "near death" are mentioned in chapter five.)

In *Session 4* Miss A said she felt as though "something" was "strangling (her) from behind like some sort of tourniquet". I asked her whether she knew anything about her birth and whether it had been made difficult as a result of the cord having been around her neck. She said she thought the labour had been a long one but knew nothing apart from that.

Some years later, after I had resumed contact with her, Miss A was kind enough to obtain a copy of her mother's obstetrical records for me. They showed that the labour had lasted 6½ hours, but there was no mention of the cord having been around the baby's neck. (Only later did I ask myself whether Miss A could have been telling me about an unconscious memory of having felt "strangled" by an insufficiently dilated cervix, her head having in that case presumably got through but not her body: the obstetrical records were to show a normal presentation.)[1] They also showed that the mother had had 6 miscarriages in the space of 7 years before Miss A's older sister was born, and that when she had become pregnant with Miss A about 18 months later, she had not been aware of being with child until the pregnancy was already in its fifth month. In the session I am reporting now, Miss A also told me that when her mother had become pregnant again some time after having had her, she had had the pregnancy terminated; on learning about this years later, she (Miss A) had "yelled" at her mother (sic): "You're a murderer, you have killed a child".

In *Session 7* I told Miss A about the result of an ENT examination that the therapeutic team had suggested I should perhaps arrange for her to have at our local general hospital concerning some repeated nose-bleeds. The specialist had written back to say that he had found some excoriations of the mucous membrane that could have been caused by self-inflicted injuries, but that he could not be sure. I questioned Miss A about this in the session, but she denied having done anything to herself. She then went on to say, in a half self-conscious and half amused sort of way, that during some of these nose-bleeds she had been swallowing the blood that trickled down her throat, and that one of the nurses, who had been attending to her at the time, had jokingly said to a patient who happened to be standing by: "Look at Dracula's daughter having her blood-meal." Swallowing her blood, Miss A continued, gave her a feeling of "living off [her]self", and with the same half amused and half self-conscious smile as before she explained that it was "easier to do this than attack other people"—by which I understood her to mean that it was easier to "live off" her own blood than "attack" other people to "live off" theirs. She also said—although this time in a more serious and factual sort of tone—that when swallowing her blood, she had derived additional comfort from spinning one of her imaginary cocoons around herself.

As this second mention of the "cocoon" had figured in a context that now contained references to "blood-meals" and "living off" one's own body because it was "easier to do this than attack other people", I returned to what I had interpreted earlier as a possible prenatal level of functioning and relatedness, but now made this a little more explicit than before by describing the transference as a foetal, blood-dependent, object-directed and aggressive form of relatedness to me, the frustrated aggressivity of which Miss A found it easier to deal with, between sessions, by deflecting it on to her own body and hence "living off" her own blood instead of that of others.

My interpretation was as follows. I told Miss A that when she phantasied herself as living inside me as in a "cocoon" during sessions, a foetally regressed part of herself felt sufficiently "safe" with me to be able to "live off", so to speak, and without fear of retaliation, the "blood" of my words, care and attention; but when the end of the session caused the "cocoon"/me to be opened and the phantasied umbilical link with me to be severed, the life-and-death quality of her foetal dependence on blood made it imperative for her to immediately find another "body" to sustain her. When it came to "other people", however, and to what I had referred to earlier as the "harsher world" of postnatal reality, she was not quite as sure of these "other people" or of this "harsher world" as she was of me or our sessions. She had said at our first meeting that "everyone in the hospital" had "got it in" for her, and this, I suggested, made her afraid of directing at the people in the hospital community the full force of her foetal cravings, lest this caused them to retaliate or to be "destroyed". (I reminded her here of a fear she had expressed, in the first admission, of having "destroyed" her parents.) Rather, therefore, than "attack" these "other people" to get some of *their* "blood", she found it easier, between sessions, to withdraw into her cocoon and get the blood from her own body. In other words, I tried to convey to Miss A my impression that what she probably wanted of me was that I not only provide a peaceful, cocoon-like place inside which she could live and feel "safe" and "completely [her]self", but that I also offer myself to her as a prenatal mother "object" on which she could exercise and satisfy the aggressive as well as the libidinal aspects of some unresolved and persistent foetal drive. I added that her anorexia could also point to a wish to revert to an umbilical, as opposed to an oral, mode of feeding.

Miss A seemed to have taken in what I had said but made no reply. Within two days of that particular session, however, the nosebleeds stopped, and I began to get reports from the nursing staff that in addition to needing a little less encouragement to eat, Miss

A was beginning to show signs of coming out of her withdrawal and of talking to people a little more, not just to me in my office.

Using this information a few sessions later (for she herself had not reported any change), I told Miss A that if my talking to her about her unresolved prenatal cravings had played any part in this change (something of which I said I could not be sure), it may be because these cravings had been sufficiently recognized for her not to have to act them out in order to draw attention to them and have them attended to; and that whatever the explanation for the change, she seemed to have made some sort of move, notwithstanding her remaining disinclination to eat, towards a slightly more open, visible, and hence presumably postnatal way of functioning and relating.

Without my saying anything to Miss A about this, I was also interested in the fact that although her emergence from the previous withdrawal had been followed by her making more open demands on the nursing staff, the latter had seemed to prefer this to the strain and frustration of seeing her withdraw from them. When I began to write up Miss A's case for the purposes of this book, I wondered whether a possible explanation for the nurses' apparent welcoming of these more open demands could be found in what she was much later to say about her mother having a kind of "strength" that was "insidious", and "dangerous as a result of not being open". If we think of what could equally be described as the "insidious", hidden, and "dangerous" way in which Miss A had deceived her personal nurse in the first admission, could one say that the nurses had now been reassured by Miss A's new and more "open" way of relating to them? Had this new way also made them feel that they now had a newborn baby to nurse instead of one who had kept hiding itself in a cocoon or the phantasied "womb" of her therapist in sessions? As I was soon to realize, however, my belief that Miss A had emerged from her prenatal regression probably owed more to wishful thinking than to a cool appraisal of the facts.

My first inkling that this was perhaps so came from Miss A's failure to make any kind of response to some patently oral material that seemed to offer a clear and satisfying explanation for the difficulty she was still having in accepting those of my interpretations that dealt with what I saw as the negative but still unconscious aspects of her feelings about me and the sessions. I had taken the emergence of this oral material as a sign that she was indeed probably beginning to relate at a more postnatal level, but its failure to respond to interpretation made me wonder whether this could be due to some remaining and prenatal kind of attachment that had not yet been worked through. My suspicions were to be confirmed by Sessions 15 and 16.

Session 15 started by Miss A telling me that she felt like "carving [her]self up with razor blades". "They"—meaning the people in the hospital community—were "trying to get inside [her] cocoon", and she had to "tighten it" in self defence. She had, however, obtained a measure of relief from one of the nurses—the same nurse, incidentally, as the one who, on seeing Miss A swallow the blood of her nose-bleeds, had jokingly referred to her as "Dracula's daughter having her blood-meal" (Session 7). This nurse had once again joked with her and asked her if she could swim, and on being told that she could, had said that in that case Miss A couldn't be "all bad", since otherwise she "would have sunk". The nurse had not been "too flippant" or "too gushing", had not "swamped" her or tried to give her "high ideals". She had made her laugh, and it had helped. (I have been wondering since then whether Miss A had sometimes enjoyed light-hearted conversations with her sister and whether, if so, this had provided a welcome relief from what I imagine must have been the more serious approach of her parents. Had the nurse similarly provided this welcome and "sisterly" kind of relief from the more serious and perhaps over-serious approach of the "parents"/me?)

I said that this was perhaps how she (Miss A) wanted me to treat her myself: to adopt a light-hearted, semi-joking stance with her, make fun in a nice way of what frightened her; not try to get inside the cocoon of idealization inside which she took refuge; abstain from what she possibly experienced as my "swamping" her with comments about a supposedly negative side of her relationship with me; and, above all, stop referring to what I thought she may be experiencing as the more persecutory aspects of a phantasied prenatal "swamp"/me, since my doing this only seemed to increase, not only her fear of it, but also, perhaps, her suicidal wish to sink further into it. Miss A listened, head slightly bowed, but said nothing.

I have also asked myself since then whether the nurse had perhaps unwittingly perceived, in what could be described as yet another stroke of intuition, what I had deduced to be the possibly foetal elements of Miss A's psychopathology. Had the nurse, for example, unconsciously perceived: (a) that since Miss A could swim, this meant that if her therapy took her back to the womb, her ability to swim would stand her in good stead and stop her from sinking to her death in the amniotic waters of her regression and of the therapy; and (b) that this would then make it impossible to regard Miss A as "all bad", since she would have shown herself to have enough "good" in her to want to fight for her survival and cooperate with the efforts made on her behalf to stop her from drowning. If, on the other hand, she could not swim and was, moreover, determined to sink and possibly take the rescuer down with her,[2] then this might cause people to see her as "bad" and thus have an adverse effect on their willingness or determination to help her.

A little later in this Session 15 Miss A said she felt that I was trying to make her "afraid of death", but that she wasn't "afraid" because she didn't "care any more about dying". This was then immediately followed by her saying that although she got "very angry" with herself when she kept people "at a distance" by withdrawing into her cocoon, she also experienced a "sense of excitement" when they "tried to know" what she was thinking. I said that notwithstanding whatever fear she may have that I too might try to get inside her mind and whatever "sense of excitement" she may also be getting from hiding inside her cocoon and not letting me see what she was thinking, the very fact that she was sharing these rather private thoughts with me must mean that she was letting at least some of me inside the cocoon. "Yes", she said, "I spin the cocoon around you too, and I also come into the corridor at night"—the corridor that led to the therapists' offices—"to try and disappear into your room".

I was intrigued by that part of Miss A's rejoinder which mentioned her spinning the cocoon around me and hence not simply around herself, as I had understood her to do until then. It seemed to mean that she now phantasied me as being inside the cocoon with her, and this was rather different from what I had previously taken to be her wish for me to *be* the cocoon, have her *inside me* and thus be the container rather than the contained. I first wondered whether her spinning the cocoon around me as well as herself was an attempt to make me into some kind of imaginary twin that would keep her company inside the womb, but this did not produce any response; nor was there any means of ascertaining whether she could have been the survivor of an undiagnosed twin pregnancy, the other twin having presumably died *in utero* and been subsequently resorbed. I did not exclude this possibility but then remembered that phantasies or dreams of sharing a uterine sort of environment with some kind of companion or object had caused certain writers to raise the question of whether this companion or object could represent an unconsciously remembered placenta (Lietaert Peerbolte, 1951, 1952; Mott, 1964, p. 310).[3] I therefore shared this thought with Miss A and said: (a) that her spinning the cocoon around me as well as herself could mean that she wanted me to be inside it with her, and that unless of course she had been the member of a twin pregnancy in which her twin had died and been resorbed before it could be detected, this intrauterine "me" could perhaps be regarded as a now unconsciously remembered and re-experienced placental kind of companion; and (b) that the role of womb, which I had previously thought to be played by myself, could now perhaps be regarded as being played mainly by my office, with her and me inside it as some kind of foetus/placenta couple. It did not at this stage occur to me that in that case the rest of the hospital community, which I had previously regarded as possibly representing the harsher world of postnatal reality, could now perhaps more accurately and plausibly be deemed to represent the surrounding body of the prenatal mother, which protects both the womb and its contents from the outside world. I return to this possibility below.

After I had voiced my suggestion that the "me" that Miss A seemed to phantasy as being inside the cocoon with her could perhaps represent an unconsciously remembered placenta, there was a brief pause that cannot have lasted more than a few seconds, but what Miss A said when she resumed did not, as far as I could see, give any indication of what her inner response had been to my comment. (The possible "father" connotations of the "me" inside the cocoon and the possibility that the "close" relationship that Miss A had had with her father as a child had perhaps in some way enabled her to feel reunited with the placental part of her unborn self that she had lost at birth did not occur to me until much later.)

Miss A said that most of the nurses saw her as "all bad", but that "here" was "different"—"here" being my office as opposed to the rest of the hospital community. "In fact", she went on, the nurses were "right", she *was* "all bad", she *knew* she was; she couldn't "even go to church"; she was "dead already", "full of badness", "full of death". I asked her what she had meant by saying that "here" was "different". Her reply was that I did not seem "as cynical as the others". The "others" seemed to be the other people in the rest of the hospital, and I must have said something about her need to keep me "good" by putting the "bad" in these "others", for her next remark was: "Yes, I put the good into you".

The session had to end there. Her inability to go to church is taken up later.

Session 16

It started with Miss A saying: "I don't like this; I feel trapped; there are so many things I want to say but it has all dried up." ... "It has built inside my head as if it's going to burst." ... "Everything is closing in on me." ... "I have to dodge...." "The more they chase, the more I have to invent." ... "It's a vicious circle that is tightening all the time." I asked her who were the people she had referred to as "they". It was the nurses: they were "forming a circle" around her that was "bearing down" on her, getting "smaller and smaller", "closing in" on her; and they were doing this to "squeeze [her] out of the hospital", "suffocate" and even "kill" her; and she added: "... and they'll get you too in the end if you're not careful".

I told Miss A that a feeling of being "squeezed out" of a contracting circle that was "bearing down" on her and getting "smaller and smaller" seemed to me to evoke birth. (At birth, the mother's cervix dilates, of course, and hence becomes larger and larger, not "smaller and smaller"; but the point of view of the unborn child's experience of it, this cervix could indeed be experienced as becoming "smaller and smaller" and "tighter and tighter"—as in Miss A's earlier reference in Session 4 of second admission to the feeling of being strangled as if by some kind of "tourniquet".)

Patient A had perhaps retained in her unconscious the memory of a painful birth experience, and this was now being re-experienced in the form of what she felt to be the "closing in" circle of the nurses. (The possibility that instead of birth Miss A may have been reliving a prenatal experience of threatened miscarriage, or even perhaps of an abortive attempt on her life, did not occur to me at the time.) I drew her attention, however, to her having started the session with the words: "I don't like this, I feel trapped", and I suggested that the word "this" could have unwittingly referred to the session itself. Miss A again shook her head in denial, thus indicating that she did not experience the "circle" as having anything to do with my interpretations, it applied only to the nurses.

It also occurred to me that what Miss A had said at the beginning of this session (16) about her feeling "chased" by the nurses and constantly having to "dodge" or defend herself against them by "tightening the cocoon" might also apply to the way in which she tried to keep me "good" by denying—that is, "dodging"—any reference I made to what I saw as the unconscious and persecutory aspects of the transference; and that if she put as much energy and determination into tightening her cocoon against my interpretations, as she did when trying to protect herself from the nurses, she herself must be unwittingly creating around herself a "suffocating" and lethal kind of "trap" which put at risk the vulnerable "foetal" part of herself as surely as she felt the nurses to be doing themselves. I shared this thought with Miss A and her response was immediate: "Yes, but a trap made by oneself is still safer than one made by others".

Taking the above thought one step further still, it also seemed to me that if the "me" around which she spun her cocoon could be regarded as an unconsciously remembered placenta, Miss A must unconsciously be also feeling that her tightening the cocoon was putting at risk, not only the life of her unborn self, but that of this "placenta"/me as well—a "me" whose importance to her, as I try to show below, seemed to lie not only in the fact that it provided her with a comforting presence and companion in the commonly shared security of the cocoon, but also in the fact that she seemed to need it as some sort of link between her and the rest of the hospital community—a link that, I thought, was to show signs of being just as essential to her as the link that the placenta provides between the foetus and the inside of the mother's body.[4] Supposing, therefore, that Miss A's unconscious had vaguely sensed that what she was doing to herself by tightening her cocoon was also being done to the "placenta"/me, could this explain what she had said on an earlier occasion: namely, that her hiding inside her cocoon might be making me "angry"? I cannot imagine that in spite of what she had once described as her tendency to look for people who could "put up with anything" she demanded of them, this would have included an expectation that my wish to help her would have gone to the length of my being prepared to die with her. She may therefore have phantasied me as not casting a very favourable eye on the fact that the means by which she chose to defend herself were putting at risk the life of the placental "me" inside the cocoon as well as that of her own foetal self.

Patient A had described the persecutory "circle" of nurses as "bearing down" on her, and I had interpreted this as the *phantasy* of an expelling womb or prenatal mother. One may remember, however, the way in her first admission the nurses had reacted to her suicidal gesture of retaliation against her personal nurse for not seeing through the falseness of her twice-repeated assurance that she could wait for half an hour before being attended to: they had closed ranks against her and played a part in her discharge. Miss A may therefore have experienced this discharge as having in reality been expelled from the womb of an angry nursing-staff/"mother". (This is taken up again below where I examine whether the nursing staff "body" could in fact on that occasion be said to have reacted, in its countertransference and not just in Miss A's phantasy, like a mother in labour in the throes of a threatened miscarriage.)

Something else that could be asked is this: In the first admission Miss A had given me the impression of doing her best to convince herself that she experienced her sessions and my office as a safe place where she could find a refuge from the rest of the hospital community; and I had assumed the latter to represent for her the harsher world of postnatal reality. Now, however, because of the seemingly uterine and obstetrical connotations of the words she had used to describe the ever narrowing "circle" she felt the nurses to be forming around her in order to "bear down" on her and "squeeze" her out of the hospital, I had had to replace this initial view by one in which she would be deemed to be unconsciously experiencing this community—and particularly the nurses who played such an important role in its containing and holding function—as an expelling sort of womb or inside of the mother's body. It could therefore be asked why I had not tried to see whether the transference could not have been interpreted at that point as one that had simply split and polarized itself along the lines of the good womb/bad womb kind of dichotomy that Melanie Klein (1957, p. 492) had suggested may well precede and "foreshadow" the "good breast"/"bad breast" one. In other words, why had I not interpreted my office and me, on the one hand, and the nursing staff and the rest of the hospital community on the other, as, respectively, the "good" (in the sense of holding, safe and friendly), and "bad" (hostile and expelling) halves of a split "womb" or "prenatal mother" imago?

Looking back, I am almost certain that the reason I did not even think of interpreting the transference in that way had been my interest in whether the "me" whom Miss A seemed to want to be inside the cocoon with her ("Yes, I spin the cocoon around you too") could represent an unconsciously remembered placenta. This interest was eventually to become responsible for my thinking that when looking at things from a prenatal angle, the transference had probably taken the form of a tripartite kind of relatedness—that is, one in which the nursing staff and the hospital community, instead of representing the harsher world of postnatal reality, as I had initially assumed, would be unconsciously perceived by Miss A as the surrounding and sometimes hostile body of the pregnant mother. My office, in turn, would be perceived and expected by her to function as a smaller, privileged, womb-like enclosure within that body, and I myself, within that enclosure, would be deemed to be unconsciously expected by Miss A not only to provide her with a comforting and placenta-like presence and extension of herself during sessions and in her "cocoons" between them, but to also function as an active and here again placental kind of link between her and the "body" of the "prenatal mother"/hospital, in the same way as the unborn child's placenta enables it to relate to and grow within the body of the pregnant mother.

This amended view of the transference—one in which the harsher world of postnatal reality would no longer be deemed to be represented by the hospital community but, rather, by the world *outside* the hospital—seems more acceptable than the previous one, for Miss A must presumably have realized that however persecutory she had often felt the hospital community to be, it was still offering some kind of protection and escape from the realities, stresses, and responsibilities of the outside world. It also seems to me that this amended view—provided, of course, one looked at the transference from a prenatal angle—would have offered some explanation for the kind of risk that Miss A had felt me to be exposing myself to by helping her. This risk had been that of being expelled by the nursing "body" (my word), and also that of possible "suffocation" and even "death". Miss A's warning to me to be "careful" lest the nursing "circle" "get [me] too in the end" may therefore have come from some unconscious association with the fact that the placenta is eventually subjected to the same forces of expulsion as the foetus itself and also "dies" shortly after being expelled.

Reflecting about all this when writing up Miss A's case made me realize that there could have been several other, this time postnatal, ways in which the material of this Session 16 could have been interpreted. One of these could have consisted in telling Miss A that she wanted me to be the loved and obviously loving father of her childhood; that she unconsciously perceived the nurses as jealous mothers who wanted to "get" both her and this "father"/me for excluding them; and that her perceiving them as mothers who would be prepared to go to the length of actually "suffocating" and "killing" both father and daughter for doing this to them could be explained by supposing that she had attributed to the nurses the murderous type of jealousy that she was later to acknowledge freely in herself. In Session 24 of this second admission, for example, she was to talk of wanting to "stab" one of my other patients "in the back"; and on another occasion she was to say: "When I lose control, everything goes, and I could kill". An interpretation along those lines would probably have made more sense to Miss A than references to wombs and placentas, and her warning that I should be "careful" lest the nurses "get [me] too in the end" could have been interpreted as her warning a "father"/me to be mindful of the possible murderous intent of jealous nursing "wives" or "mothers". Such an interpretation would, admittedly, have been incomplete, ignoring as it would have done the apparently obstetrical connotations of a contracting "circle", of the "squeezing out" and "bearing down" terminology and of the placental image of a "me" who was inside the "circle" with her. But my experience has been that even when a certain type of material seems to invite or even require an interpretation on prenatal lines, it is equally important to immediately look for and interpret what will almost always be its postnatal counterpart. There is, of course, nothing new in this notion that a given event or situation can not only be experienced by a patient but also require an interpretation by the therapist simultaneously at two different levels, either equally or with one level being more strongly defined than the other. I have in fact asked myself whether what I am discussing here is in some way similar to what Grotstein had in mind when putting forward his "Siamese-twin" or "dual-track" theory of mental development and functioning (1981, pp. 87–89, 1983a, p. 412, 1983b, p. 492). Bion himself (1962) seems to have seen no difficulty in conceiving of situations that could be experienced in different ways, and at different levels, simultaneously.

Assuming that the postnatal levels of the interaction between Miss A and me could be said to have been underscored by a mother/unborn child kind of interaction, I have tried to imagine how it might in retrospect be possible to describe the unconscious hopes and expectations that Miss A may have had concerning what the hospital might be able to do for her unborn self and her "placenta"/me if things had proceeded in an ideal sort of way—that is, the way in which events normally unfold when a pregnancy is following a favourable and uneventful course. Had an unresolved and still active foetal part of Miss A unconsciously hoped to find in the hospital a place that would, for example, have been able to do for her something like the following:

1. protect her from the outside world and keep her warm in the form of central heating as well as human "warmth", containment and care, in the same way as the pregnant mother's body performs these functions for the unborn child;

CLINICAL MATERIAL   61

2. offer, within that body, a separate, privileged, womb-like enclosure in the form of a therapist's office, and provide, inside that office, a therapist who, in addition to being willing to act as a placenta-like extension of her own thoughts and feelings and as a pleasant and supportive presence in the "womb" of that office, would also function as an indispensable link as well as a semi-permeable barrier between her and the rest of the hospital community/"prenatal mother", thus making it possible for her to benefit from this "mother" without feeling too "attacked" by the latter in one form or another;

3. maintain, in the phantasized "womb" of the therapist's office and mainly as a result of the "placenta"/therapist's protective and detoxifying function, a good consulting-room "atmosphere" as well as an adequate supply of nourishing love and food for thought—that is, good "oxygen" and nutrients, uncontaminated by the "poison" of other people's real or imagined hostility, or by too much accent being put on the negative side of the transference (a point that has been touched on already);

4. generally constitute a place in which, when she was back in the rest of the hospital community between sessions and hence had to rely on her own "psychological placenta" (I explain below what I mean by Miss A's own "psychological placenta") to survive in it until the next session, she could find a good "atmosphere"[5] and a place that would be able to receive, tolerate, and dispose of both her and her therapist's own waste products: of all the anxieties, bad moods, and unwanted feelings that not only patients but also therapists often relieve themselves of in the hospital community when under stress in one form or another;

5. contain and hold Miss A and her "placenta"/therapist until Miss A had reached "term" and was ready for "birth"—that is, discharge—and until the "placenta"/therapist, having outlived its usefulness, could be safely discarded.[6]

At the time, the main significance of Session 16 seemed to me to lie in the fact that whereas Miss A's material had not until then given any sign of her carrying in her mind an unconscious memory or image of the womb other than that suggested by her mention, in the first admission, of her self-made cocoons—that is, the image of a place of peace and tranquillity in which she could, in her own words, feel "safe and completely [her]self"—a very different picture seemed to have been created by what she had said in Session 16 about an ever-narrowing "circle" of nurses that was "bearing down" on her, which I had interpreted as a womb or prenatal mother in labour, which, she felt, was trying to "squeeze [her] out of the hospital" or even "kill" her. More importantly still, perhaps, this same session (Session16) had also shown a change in the way she experienced the cocoon itself. The latter, too, was now a place where her life was being threatened. She had tried to "pretend" to herself that she still felt "safe" inside it, but it hadn't "worked", and she now had to admit that even in the cocoon, "death" was trying to "get" her. She had not, admittedly, gone as far as to explicitly admit to herself, let alone to me, that a similar change had also taken place in the way she experienced her sessions, but one may recall that she had started Session 16 with the words: "I don't like this, I feel trapped", and that this had been one of the reasons for my taking the view, and my telling Miss A, that in spite of her denial she probably did feel closed in upon by a trapping circle of interpretations as well as by a constricting "circle" of nurses.

I indicated earlier that the material of Session 16 might enable me to give another—this time prenatal—rendering to what Miss A had mentioned in Session 15 as her inability to "even go to church". Perhaps I can now explain what I had in mind.

Session 30 was to suggest that the "ideal mother" for whom Miss A had once said she searched was not restricted to being a "womb-mother", with the latter's usual "cliché" connotations of perfect and blissful love, but that Miss A had also felt in need of a postnatal mother who could combine compassion with firmness and even, if necessary, punishment. Notwithstanding this, her search had also been for a mother in whom she could find some intra-uterine kind of refuge and feeling of security, away from what she so often appeared to experience as the harsh injustice of a loveless and postnatal sort of world. If we now think, therefore, of the "asylum" and "sanctuary" function that the inside of churches used to sometimes perform in medieval times, and also of the sense of peace and isolation from the outside world that even nonbelievers sometimes get from just sitting in a half-empty church when a service is not in progress, could one suppose (this has most probably been suggested already anyway), that the inside of a church can become associated in the unconscious with what our need for idealization often causes us to fondly believe it must have been like to be in our mother's womb? And if so, could one suppose that the feelings of guilt and unworthiness (she had felt "all bad") that had presumably prevented Miss A from entering a church had included a fear that if she did enter this idealized mother's body, this would be just the moment when a phantasied and punishing mother, incensed by what she saw as her daughter's appropriation of her (the mother's) husband, had been waiting for to close in upon her like a clam and destroy her? One could perhaps evoke here Melanie Klein's suggestions concerning the possible role played by phantasies of "entering the mother's body" and the fear of being "imprisoned and persecuted within it" (1946, p. 305), as well as Chasseguet-Smirgel's own thoughts concerning the possible prenatal origins of the Oedipus complex (1984a, p. 171; 1984b; 1990, p. 79; 1992).

The remaining 35 sessions of "Miss A's second admission showed a marked improvement in her relationship with some of the nurses, two of whom she found particularly helpful. There were also several other instances of what I took to be the transference's prenatal features, but to mention them all would, I think, be tedious. I shall therefore end here my description of Miss A's transference and turn to countertransference considerations. The reactions she had evoked in me and the rest of the staff at the end of her first admission seemed to me particularly worth examining and were to lead to a few thoughts about the effect on countertransference of prenatally regressed patients in general.

Before I go into this, however, perhaps I can briefly return and add something to what I said earlier about the resistance one often encounters to interpretations offered at prenatal level. I mentioned the possible usefulness, in such cases, of first trying to see whether the material can also be interpreted on postnatal lines, the hope being that this will make more sense to the patient and hence prepare the ground for a possible reference to the prenatal underscoring later. Another way, it seems to me, of handling this sort of resistance is to remind oneself of one of the frequently encountered reasons for patients' resistance to interpretations in general—a reason that, if the patient could put it into words, would consist in saying to the therapist: "I don't want you to interpret that I have this or that desire, I want you to satisfy it; I want the real thing, not some comment about my wanting it." A patient who was usually extremely punctual did not on one occasion arrive for his usual session; he telephoned me half an hour or so later, very upset and apologetic, saying he had completely forgotten his appointment and had only remembered it when enjoying the cooling comfort of his swimming pool (it was a very hot summer afternoon). His usual reaction to prenatal interpretations had been of the type mentioned earlier: "It doesn't get me anywhere." ... "What can I do with it?" I told him that he had perhaps preferred the enjoyment of the real amniotic swimming pool to a possible interpretation of his wanting it. He was a very intelligent man, but I am not sure that he was convinced.

The countertransference implications and countertransference to prenatally regressed patients in general

Various writers (Burger-Piaget, 1973; Paul, 1983; A. Rascovsky et al., 1971b; Share, 1994) have shown their interest in the effect that prenatally regressed patients could sometimes be said to have on the countertransference of the individual analyst in what seems to have been a one-to-one and outpatient kind of setting. Working with inpatients gives the opportunity of dealing with particularly severe forms of prenatal regression, and although Patient A's case was an isolated case, I thought it might be worth trying to see whether it, too, could have told us something about the occasional effect on the individual therapist as well as on a whole therapeutic team and, indeed, other hospital staff, of dealing with a prenatally regressed patient.

To examine this point, I shall go back to the interaction that had taken place between Miss A and ourselves in the last 48 hours of her first admission. At the time, all I had seen was what could be described as the "postnatal" aspects of the total staff countertransference: how the nurses, in closing ranks against Miss A, could, for example, be said to have unwittingly taken on the role of the disapproving grandparents; how Miss A's personal nurse had been made to play that of the favoured granddaughter who, in the eyes of the grandparents, could apparently do no wrong; how the head of the Unit had been put in the unenviable position of having to declare himself unable to support Miss A's wish to continue to attend her sessions with me (which had probably represented for her something like the university she had wanted to attend); and how my own reaction had been to unwittingly take on the role of a supportive but ineffectual mother who had done her best to counteract the hostility of this nursing "grandparents" but had failed in the attempt.

At the time I had, of course, no idea of the extent and intensity of Miss A's prenatal regression, which started to show itself only during the first few weeks of the second admission. On the other hand, it seems reasonable to assume that it was already present, and doing its work, silently and unobtrusively, right from the start. If we therefore remember Sessions 7, 15, and 16 of this second admission, particularly what seems to have been the obstetrical implications of Session 16, could we suppose that when Miss A had described the nurses as forming a "circle" that was "bearing down" on her in an attempt to "squeeze" her out of the hospital and even "kill" her, she was in effect unwittingly letting me know how their reaction to her suicidal acting out in the first admission had been unconsciously experienced by her at the time as some kind of threatened miscarriage or deliberate abortive attempt? Could one go even further? Could the nursing "body", feeling attacked in a sensitive part of itself (its womb, represented by Miss A's nurse), be said to have reacted in reality to this attack by contracting around Miss A like a womb in the throes of a premature labour or threatened miscarriage? And since Miss A had added that if I wasn't "careful" the nurses would "get (me) too in the end", could she be said to have unconsciously seen in me a kind of human placenta that would, as a result of being "attached" to her both physically and emotionally, itself be in danger of being expelled from the hospital with her or soon after her?—and if not from the hospital, at least from the respect and good will of a therapeutic team of which I wanted to remain a member? In other words, had what I outlined earlier as a foetal or prenatal form of transference evoked in Miss A's case what would be called a puerperal or prepuerperal from of total staff countertransference?

Regarding this notion of my being, placenta-like, in some kind of danger, I do in fact clearly remember what I had felt at the time: as soon as I realized that the whole situation had become too difficult for us to handle, I had quickly disengaged myself from Miss A emotionally (at least superficially) and had arranged for her transfer back to the psychiatric hospital. The pre- or perinatal implications of this had not yet been fully worked out, and I had reacted purely instinctively, but when looking at things from a pre- and perinatal point of view, one could say that I must have unconsciously realized that my failure to disengage from my patient emotionally might result in my losing my own placental "adhesion" to the uterine wall of a hospital or team "mother" that was showing signs of no longer being able or willing to contain its patient.

Although Miss A's case had been an isolated one, the above attempt to understand how her unresolved prenatal cravings could have influenced the way we had all reacted to her suicidal acting out at the end of her first admission[7] was to result in yet another and more general train of thought.

I was thinking one day about Simmel's observation that patients treated in hospital "by psychoanalysis" tended to "identify the clinic" with the "hidden intra-uterine existence" (1929, p. 86), when it occurred to me that patients' relatives or even members of the general public sometimes use the term "rebirth" to describe what they hope will be the successful outcome, on discharge, of a psychologically ill patient's admission to hospital for psychotherapy. Admittedly, those who talk of "rebirth" in this context often do so in jest, treating it as something of a joke, and their doing this usually seems to be yet another example of the facetious type of humour often used as a defence against the anxiety aroused by anything psychiatric.[8] On the other hand, the very word "rebirth" seems to show that some association has taken place, in the minds of those who used it, between spending a few months in hospital for psychotherapy and the few months that the patient had spent inside the mother's body before being "discharged" at birth—as if the "cure" consisted of going back into that body for a little while in order to come out of it "reborn" and ready for a "new beginning". I again borrow these last two words from Balint, even though he used it to describe the favourable outcome of emerging, not from a prenatal form of regression, but from a proper working through of what he called the stage of "primary object-love", conceived by him as the "very earliest state of extra-uterine mental life" (1937, p. 103).

It then occurred to me that to use, even in jest, this term "re-birth" to describe the outcome of a few months in hospital for inpatient psychotherapy presupposes some degree of conscious or unconscious belief in the patient's admission having constituted some sort of "impregnation", by the referrer, of a hospital/"mother"; and although this idea seemed at first rather incongruous, it resulted in a train of thought that has been with me ever since.

Posing this idea of an "impregnation" of the hospital by the referrer as some kind of premise, I first asked myself whether the first few weeks following admission, when no one knows for certain whether the patient is going to be able to stay and settle, could be compared to the seven to nine days that are assumed to elapse between the fertilization of the human egg and the latter's "implantation", or "embedding", into the endometrial stroma (an inpatient is sometimes referred to as a "bed" patient). I then found, to my surprise, that the analogy could be followed further. We know, for example, that even if the egg does succeed in getting embedded in the uterine wall, much will depend on the manner in which it interacts with the host mother after that. The latter's body may for conscious or unconscious reasons be unable or unwilling to continue with the pregnancy; the embryo itself, depending on the strength of its life-force, may or may not be able (or willing?) to survive the conditions offered to it. In other words, the pregnancy may or may not "take". I asked myself whether this could be repeated in the sort of patient/staff interaction that takes place during the two to four weeks' "trial" admission, which enables an institution (such as the one from which my observations have been drawn) to give both patient and staff the opportunity to get to know each other before deciding whether they wish to continue.

Going on from there, we also know that even if the trial admission does end with a formal offer of further treatment and with the patient's acceptance of this offer, much will still depend on how patient and hospital "get on" with each other from then on. If the therapy proceeds satisfactorily, a time may come when members of the therapeutic team begin to feel the patient to be "moving", to be more "in contact" with them, and when they experience pleasure from this. Could this reaction be compared, I again asked myself, with the so-called "quickening" sensation experienced by the pregnant mother when she begins to feel the child to be "moving" inside her and when she, too, if she looks forward to having a child, experiences pleasure from this sensation? A little later still, the team may feel that the patient is strong enough for one to be able to envisage a return to the outside world: could that be compared to the time when the pregnant mother and her womb begin to exert slight but increasing pressure on the foetus as the latter keeps on growing—a pressure that will eventually climax in the final "push" of birth or, in the case of hospital work, "discharge"? Was it also mere coincidence that in most cases it was not considered healthy for a patient to remain an "in"-patient for more than a few months; that during the weeks before discharge, birth dreams and phantasies were not an uncommon finding; and that if there were signs that a patient was going to be harmed by being allowed to remain an inpatient for too long, his or her discharge was sometimes "induced" by the setting of a leaving date,[9] as in an artificially brought about "induction" of labour?

I then realized that asking myself these questions had been tantamount to envisaging the possibility that, alongside the more disturbed forms of prenatal interaction between patients and staff, there appeared to be other forms of interaction that also lent themselves to a prenatal kind of rendering but that did not, this time, appear to be particularly pathological; and I was struck by the fact that these apparently benign forms of prenatal interaction seemed to be repeating the various stages of a pregnancy that had followed a relatively uneventful course, whereas the more disturbed ones could be said to have enacted a pregnancy kind of crisis.

This, then, eventually led me to ask myself whether it might be possible to formulate a hypothesis such as the following:

1. Foetal/puerperal or foetal/prepuerperal levels of patient/staff interaction are inevitably set in motion by the admission of *any* patient entering an inpatient therapeutic community for the purpose of individual, psychoanalytically oriented therapy.

Such modes of interaction are characterized in part by the fact that in its countertransference, the staff may sometimes unwittingly respond to the frequently unrecognized foetal nature of a patient's demands and expectations by reacting to and around him or her in a way reminiscent of that in which an unborn child's immediate and not so immediate environment—the inside of the mother's body, the mother as a person, the expectant father, the rest of the family, professional attendants, and so on—sometimes respond to a pregnancy, and/or a birth, for better or worse.

2. When such an interaction is not too disturbed or difficult to handle, this may be the case of a patient whose intra-uterine life had been uneventful, or the effect of a moderately disturbed pregnancy had been compensated for by good neo-natal care, as well as by the resilience of an innately strong constitution.

3. When the said interaction is particularly disturbed and difficult to handle, this may be the case of a patient whose prenatal life had, for one reason or another—constitutional factors, placental dysfunction due to defect or injury, deficient health in the mother resulting in foetal malnutrition or exposure to noxae, etc.—not proceeded as smoothly as one might have wished, or in whom severe postnatal deprivation or trauma had succeeded in denting the experience or "memory" of a relatively undisturbed prenatal phase and in thus damaging the very foundations on which the development of a secure postnatal ego presumably depends: the danger being, in such cases, that the frequently unrecognized prenatal levels of such interaction may not only give rise to the extremely disturbed and painful form of patient–staff interaction described in an earlier work as "the bad sequence" (Ployé, 1977), but also, and worse still, become malignant.

Using words such as "benign" or "malignant" with respect to prenatal forms of regression would be doing nothing more than extend what Balint had done with respect to postnatal regressions (1968, pp. 141–146) or what G. Adler himself had done by distinguishing between "therapeutic" and "disruptive" forms of regression (1974, p. 258). Nor does the use of such notions as "benignity" and "malignancy" with respect to inpatient work do much more than extend to it Rank's pioneering observation that certain transferences repeat the "physiological connection" that had existed between mother and unborn child between conception and birth (1924, pp. 5–6). The hospital itself would then be deemed to play the role of the pregnant mother, with the therapist functioning as some "placental" kind of link between the patient and the rest of the hospital community.

Could the experience gained in hospital work contribute to one's understanding of the interaction that takes place between patient and analyst or therapist when individual therapy is carried out in the one-to-one setting of private practice or that of a hospital outpatient department or clinic?

All I can do here is to repeat one of the suggestions I made earlier, namely that in all analyses or psychoanalytically oriented therapies—that is, not just those that are conducted in an inpatient type of setting—the interaction that takes place between patient and therapist can be said to be underscored by a prenatal level of interaction in which the holding and containing function of the therapy can sometimes be seen to be unconsciously perceived and even used by the patient as a phantasied womb or prenatal mother, with the result that the therapist may unwittingly or half knowingly react to the patient in the same way that the latter's mother had reacted to him during her pregnancy. In this interaction the therapist's more interpretive, reflective, and discriminating function can be deemed to play, between the patient and the containing therapist/"prenatal mother", a role not unlike that which the patient's placenta had played in helping him relate to the inside of the pregnant mother's body. In this way of thinking, the "placental" nature of the analyst's interpretations can be regarded as a normal and non-pathological feature of the analytic work. In extreme and pathological cases, on the other hand, when the patient's dependence and helplessness causes the therapist to decide, rightly or wrongly, that the patient can no longer respond to interpretations alone and requires the therapist to act as a kind of auxiliary "ego", this could be regarded as the re-enactment of instances when the patient's placenta had not in fact functioned adequately during prenatal life. The patient could then be communicating this to the therapist by giving up all attempts to use his own—that is, the patient's own—placental "ego" and by handing over its role to the therapist for the latter to operate it in his place as some kind of "auxiliary placenta". (The way in which, from birth onwards, the rapidly developing postnatal ego—and "brain-ego" in particular—could be conceived as taking over the communicative and linking function that the placenta had carried out during the latter part of the pregnancy by enabling the unborn child to relate to the inside of the mother's body, is discussed in chapter three.) These two prenatal, relatively distinct but complementary aspects of the analytic stance could then be conceived as underscoring the way in which, at postnatal level, the "holding" and "interpreting" functions of the analyst can also be said to fulfil a respectively "maternal" (listening) and "paternal" (interpreting) kind of role. (See, in this connection, Chasseguet-Smirgel, 1992, pp. 16.)

The above remarks concerning the occasional effect on countertransference of dealing with prenatally regressed patients can, I think, best be concluded by a reference to another paper that seems to me to have come closest to my way of thinking in spite of being one in which the words "prenatal", "foetal transference", womb, intra-uterine, foetus, embryo, placenta and so on, do not even appear.

In a 1976 paper, Hochmann related how he had once tried to treat psychopathic patients in a hospital type of setting, and how he and his colleagues had come to the conclusion that the bad results obtained could perhaps be attributed to the fact that a residential type of setting "inevitably comes to play a maternal role" (p. 628; translated for this edition).

This, said Hochmann, had encouraged "parasitism" and thus led to a destructive sort of interaction between the "parasite" patients and the "host" hospital. The latter had become hostile[10] to the former and tried to reject the patients like a "foreign body" (p. 626). This counter-aggressivity of the hospital "mother", triggered off by the parasitic and insatiable demands of the patients, is described vividly throughout and with impressive clinical material. Hochmann makes it clear that he had seen those demands, acted out in the form of violent verbal attacks on the staff or wanton destructive attacks on the hospital building and its contents, as having been directed not only against a phantasied "breast"/mother (pp. 653–654, 656) but, and even more so, at the phantasied inside of the mother's body (pp. 620–621, 649). He also compared the counter-aggressivity of the staff, and of the institution as a whole, to the retaliation of a pregnant mother's body which can no longer tolerate the presence inside it of a "foreign body" (p. 626) by which it feels "poisoned" (p. 649) and against the aggression of which it can only defend itself by "rejection" (p. 626). All this seems to me almost identical, therefore, to what I have been describing here, the only difference being that the psychopathic patients mentioned by Hochmann had acted out their parasitism and aggressivity in a much more blatant, consistent, and unconcerned manner than is normally found even in the most severely disturbed type of borderline inpatients, however destructive the latter can sometimes be. Patient A herself had sometimes indulged in this kind of aggressivity. On one occasion, for example, when everyone was asleep in the hospital except for the right orderly, she had come unobserved to the consulting-room block and hurled some breakable objects at the outside wall of my office, making a dent in the plaster as well as what she was later to refer to, because of the broken pieces, as "a mess on the carpet". On another occasion, although not at night, she did the same against a wooden door; that time, much to her disappointment, the objects had not broken, but she had derived pleasure from the noise and commotion it had caused. Although the first instance of acting out, in particular, had made it impossible for her to go on pretending to me or herself that she harboured no aggressive feelings towards me, it did not tell me exactly what she had against me and/or my treatment. That became clear later.

Hochmann also related in his paper how he and his colleagues had eventually decided to see whether better results could be obtained by treating the same kind of psychopathic patients in the non-residential setting of a day centre, the hope being that this would minimize or do away with the regressive, deleterious, "maternal" effect of hospital life on the patients. With great honesty, Hochmann has made no attempt to disguise the fact that this experiment, too, led to "disillusionment" (p. 630), particularly for the staff—the patients seemed to have enjoyed their parasitic destructiveness. This was neatly summed up by Hochmann in a footnote (p. 682) by saying that whereas patients treated in hospital had become "internal parasites who had silently poisoned our institutional body" from within, those treated in the day centre behaved like "external parasites which adhered to our surface": a perfect if unwitting description, it seems to me, of a change from a foetal to an oral type of "parasitism". The frequent overlap or even fusion between an oral type of transference and a foetal one had been one of the findings made in the course of my Patient A's treatment at my old hospital. I therefore mention this paper by Hochmann as one that would appear to offer further justification for a closer study of the effect that unresolved foetal cravings can be deemed to have on countertransference, and this whether analytic work is carried out in a residential or a non-residential setting.

PATIENT "C"

Referral

This patient, to whom I shall refer as "Miss C", was referred to my old hospital for an assessment of her suitability for psychotherapy. At the time, and like my other colleague therapists, I was mostly involved with inpatient work, but each of us had to make time for a limited amount of outpatient work, and Miss C was allotted to me. I saw her for 10 outpatient sessions, at the end of which she declared herself completely recovered, expressed much gratitude, and left. Some of her material seemed to have lent itself to a prenatal line of interpreting, and this is why I am reporting it here.[11]

When referred to us, Miss C was in her late thirties, single, self-employed, and the referrer—a consultant psychiatrist at a nearby psychiatric hospital—reported that she had been complaining of depression but that she appeared to be more tense and distressed than truly depressed. He thought that what had probably precipitated her seeking help had been the breakdown of two important relationships with men in the course of the previous year. He described her personality as "driving, obsessional, forceful." The patient had told the referrer that she no longer felt able to work, but he had advised her to try to keep working if at all possible.

Session 1

I invited Miss C to sit in the chair opposite me and to tell me about her problem. She started straightaway and as though impelled by some considerable pressure and anxiety. She said she could not "go on", was losing "job after job" or walked out of them because she could no longer hold them. She felt she was facing disaster, and that if something were not done soon, she would collapse completely. Even now, she was "hanging on by a thread". It would be no use, she said, my offering her outpatient appointments. She could no longer support herself and needed to come into hospital. She added: "Nothing short of that will do any good."

She explained that all her relationships with men and women kept breaking down. She had had sexual experience with both sexes, but it was the men who had caused her most difficulties. The demands she made on them were such that after a while they could no longer tolerate her and had to end the relationship in self-defence. She inspired in them a kind of "loathing" towards her. At the beginning of each relationship, she had to make her partner into *"an extension of" herself*, she "lost [her] identity", became extremely *"demanding"*, and *"drained the man emotionally dry"*. She could never be satisfied by a man, and after intercourse she always told him so, asked for his attention all the time, and wanted to know all his thoughts. The last one, as all the others before him, had not been able to stand this and had left her. She now felt a kind of "cold emptiness" that pervaded everything. The only thing that brought her any calm was the "*sun*, the *sea*, the *tide*". It was "like an obsession, this yearning for the sun and the sea". About her demandingness and her draining the man dry, she said, "I can't stop myself, it's like a drug, *I am like a vampire, and I need this to form a relationship at all*".

At this point she stopped and seemed to expect some response from me. I had for some time been interested in the possible usefulness of postulating not only the existence, but also the interpretability, of prenatal levels of transference, and it seemed to me that some of my patient's opening remarks could perhaps be responded to with that in mind. I realized that at one level her frantic and unsuccessful search for sexual satisfaction in her relationship with men, her inability to stop herself "draining them emotionally dry", and her saying that it was "like a drug", could be regarded as stemming from some unresolved and greedy search for the mother's breast. As she seemed to be wanting to "suck" me into her way of thinking by trying to convince me that my arranging for her immediate admission to hospital was the only way of preventing a total breakdown, she could also be said to be displacing this search on to me. I shared this thought with Miss C but also told her that some of her other remarks were making me think that her trouble probably went deeper than that.

Explaining what I had in mind, I said she had made it clear that she did not want to be an outpatient but, rather, an inpatient, and that "nothing short of coming into hospital would do any good". She had also told me that she was "like a vampire"—in other words, someone who lives off other people's blood—and that she "needed this to form any relationship at all". All this, I said, suggested to me that behind the oral aspects of her greed lay a not inconsiderable amount of unresolved prenatal strivings. For there to be "any relationship at all", an unborn child had to have "blood", uninterrupted access to the source of supply—such as only inpatient care would provide—and to be "inside" somewhere. A newborn baby no longer needed the mother's blood, could tolerate breaks in the relationship with her, and no longer needed to be "inside" her: it could be an "out-baby" (outpatient). I added that what she was probably looking for in the body and mind of men was not only a penis but a "penis–umbilical cord" sort of link with them: in her own words, an "extension of [her]self"—as, indeed, the pregnant mother could be said to be in relation to her unborn child. (I failed to see that a more accurate way of giving a prenatal rendering to this search for an extension of one's "self" could have consisted in exploring the possibility that my patient may not have got over the loss of what had been the real "extension" of herself in prenatal life—namely her placenta—and that what she was looking for in men could be that erstwhile and now lost part of herself[12].)

These foetal demands, I continued, could, of course, not be met. They could only result in repeated rejections, the men eventually cutting her off from their body and getting rid of her like an abortus. The abused penis/umbilical cord kind of link was already getting frayed, and she was "hanging on by a thread".

Something in Miss C's expression told me that she had been listening intently, but by that time there were only twenty minutes left, and I went back to discussing what we should do next. I sounded her out again about her claim that nothing short of coming into hospital would help. She was adamant. Even if I could see her every day as an outpatient, it wouldn't work, she was heading for a complete breakdown. I suggested that such a breakdown might, then, be the acting out of some greedy and self-destructive rage against me for refusing admission, and that the way in which she was making a plea for immediate admission could be an instance of her demandingness towards men.

"Yes", she said, "you may well be right, but telling me this isn't any good". Yes, of course she realized she was being demanding and blackmailing towards me, but she really did need to come into hospital, and soon. If she went out of my room without knowing that there was a chance of coming into hospital, and when this was likely to be, she did not know what would happen. I weighed up the risk. There were no outpatient vacancies at the time, and my attempts to interpret her wish to come into hospital as a drive to force her way into the mother and go back to foetal life certainly did not seem to have had much effect. I therefore told her that I would recommend that her name be put on the waiting list for admission, but that I could not at this stage give her any idea of how long she would have to wait. She immediately expressed some concern about how she would manage during the interval. I told her that my inpatient and other outpatient work would make it difficult for me to give her this intermediate outpatient support myself and that I doubted if any of my colleagues who did outpatient work had any vacancies at that particular moment, but I would inquire. If my doubts were confirmed, I would get in touch with her family doctor to see what could be done and then report back to her (the patient) as soon as possible. This seemed to satisfy her, but she then expressed another anxiety. If she were admitted, did I think she might be discovered to have "something horrible" inside her, "like some kind of growth or cancer" that would frighten or "repel" other patients and cause the doctors to discharge her? All I could think of saying was that my offer to put her name on the waiting list for admission may have been unconsciously interpreted by her as a sign that her prenatal greed had already begun to eat its way into my sympathy (and confidence); that when the fertilized egg begins to eat its way into the uterine wall at "implantation", the rate at which its cells multiply has often been compared to that of cancerous cells, and that if the mother's natural defences are unable to exert some control over the invasiveness of the new growth inside her, the egg may develop into a malignant tumour instead of an embryo. If she could eat her way that easily into me, would the hospital itself be unable to keep her prenatal greed under control, with the result that the latter might then become some kind of cancer inside her, and one against which the inside of the hospital/"mother's" body would defend itself by expelling her? Could that be her fear? Miss C seemed satisfied with this explanation of her new anxiety, and the session finished on that note.

After she left, I found, as expected, that none of my colleagues were able to provide the kind of support that I had in mind. I therefore got in touch with Miss C's family doctor, said I had arranged for her to be placed on the waiting list for eventual admission, but that the present problem was that of helping her over the waiting period; and I asked the GP whether she thought her patient might be able to find the money for such help if it could be found. The doctor was a little surprised at this, expressed some doubt about Miss C's ability to find a job to pay for this, but gave me carte blanche to try to organize whatever seemed appropriate. I telephoned Miss C the following day to explain the position, and she immediately asked me whether, if private help were arranged, it could be not only with me but also on Saturdays, since she would need to look for a job and would find it difficult to be accepted for one if she said that she would need some time off during the week. It was my turn to be a little surprised, but a private patient I had been seeing on Saturday mornings had just told me she now felt sufficiently well to leave, and I therefore told Miss C that I would in fact be able to see her on Saturdays and could start straightaway if that was alright with her. It was, and I gave her an appointment for the Saturday of that same week, again at the hospital.

The remaining nine sessions

Of the other nine sessions only the last two, Sessions 9 and 10, are described in some detail. I thought brevity would best be served if I simply summed up what seemed to me to have been the main features of the intervening sessions—that is, Sessions 2 through 8.

Sessions 2–8

Without a doubt, the dominant feature that ran through all of Miss C's sessions, including the last two, was her fear of silences. I understood some of it at the time, but not all of it, and when I did eventually realize what I had missed, I almost felt like calling my patient back to tell her of my afterthought; but I had left it too late, and I decided against it.

At postnatal level, this fear of silences seemed to have had something to do with Miss C's relationship to her late father.

She had told me that when her father did not speak to her, she felt "awful". It seemed likely, therefore, that a silence during a session would have given rise in her to a fear that I had became a disapproving, uninterested, tired, or even "dead" father. I shall explain the word "dead" shortly, but I should also point out that as I found her material interesting and easy to respond to, I must have been experienced by her as a father who was interested in what his daughter had to say, the result being that the flow of talk between us had been very rarely interrupted by a silence, especially since she herself did not let these last more than a few seconds.

The first session, however, had already shown the likelihood of Miss C's psyche still being suffused with unresolved prenatal strivings. When, therefore, and in addition to this, she was to tell me in Session 8 that she had inquired about her birth and been told by her mother that it had been "terrible" and that "forceps had been used", I wondered whether some temporary interruption in the flow of blood to the brain during labour could have resulted in some degree of foetal anoxia and distress, which a prolonged silence in sessions would then have repeated. This seemed to tally with the way she had described her fear, when going to bed with a man, that she was not going to enjoy the lovemaking: "I am still petrified of a physical relationship; at the crucial moment I feel as if a plug is being pulled out, feel sadistic towards the partner. I am hoping to get cured without getting too close." My reasoning, and my interpretation, were therefore as follows.

I told Miss C that, bearing in mind the impression I had formed, in the first session, that what she was unconsciously seeking in a man's penis was some kind of umbilical cord that would attach her to him and recreate for her the feeling of being in her mother's womb, I couldn't help wondering whether the ordeal she could well have suffered during her mother's difficult labour may have conditioned her to expect that when she sought to recreate a blissful prenatal experience through sex, something might suddenly go horribly wrong there as well, and whether a silence in sessions could produce something akin to that dread. Rather, therefore, than being once again at the mercy of something over which she had had no control, did she unwittingly "pull the plug" out herself and "switch off" in order to maintain at least some degree of mastery over the situation? My notes do not tell me, nor can I recall, how Miss C responded to this attempt to make sense of her sexual difficulty. I had also been intrigued by something else Miss C had told me in that same 8th session: namely, that she "constantly swallowed during intercourse". I asked her whether she had practised oral sex on the man and swallowed the semen, but she said that she in fact lived in "constant dread" of the man asking her to take his penis in her mouth, and I had in any case often been struck by the apparent ineffectiveness, in the case of patients who were compulsive swallowers, of interpretations couched in terms of "fellatio" or "breast-sucking" phantasies. What seemed to have been the strongly prenatal tenor of Miss C's material made me more inclined to think that in the latter part of the pregnancy the foetus regulates the pressure of its amniotic fluid by periodically swallowing some of it in various amounts (Milaković, 1967, 1982). I therefore told Miss C that her swallowing during lovemaking might be regarded as the reactivation of this foetal and regulatory kind of swallowing. The session had to finish there, and there was no time to wait for a possible response.

I should now like to return to Miss C's fear of silences and say what I later thought to have been the real cause for this fear.

As early as Session 2 she had told me that a few years previously, on being told that a close female friend of hers had died in an accident, the "shock" had been "so great" that she had "laughed hysterically for a whole week". In the following session, on my discussing with her the advisability of her using the couch, she had said that if I wanted her to use the couch, she would "laugh hysterically and then cry". I failed at the time to see that if she used the couch she wouldn't be able to see me unless she turned around; that if there were no talk between us that reassured her that I was still alive, a silent me would probably be experienced as having suddenly "died" on her; and that this "dead" me could quite easily be associated in her unconscious with a fear of having drained me of all my blood by what she had described in the first session as her "vampire"—like greed for men's assurances of love.

In Session 6, she did in fact persuade herself to use the couch (it was "silly not to try"), and at some point there was a short silence, which she broke by saying: "The silence is giving me nausea. If I take my feet off the bottom when I swim, I shall go berserk." I said she needed to feel my presence with the "feet" of her words, and that a silence produced a fear of sinking. I also thought of Mott's observation that the foetus could be said to "tread" the "bottom" of the womb by means of its two umbilical arteries (1964, p. 322), but I made no comment. I simply said that "feeling" me with the "feet" of her words may also be reassuring her that she was not going to be sucked back into what she may be phantasying as an exhausted or even dying prenatal mother/me who, in order to come back to life herself, needed to take back from her all the life and blood she had unconsciously felt to be taking from me. Segal has described this kind of fear in her analysis of a schizophrenic patient (1956, p. 340).

Now for Sessions 9 and 10.

Session 9

"The couch no longer worries me so much. I have no need for a binding relationship. My friend asked me to share his life. I calmly refused. Before, I would have gone for any man, anything to have an envelope, warm and cosy, anyone who would bind me up. Now I go to bed with him quite cheerfully. It's wonderful. I enjoy sex for the first time in my life, and I am fully satisfied. My ESP is also increasing, but I still can't bear to think of my friend who got killed."

I made the obvious connection between her enjoying sex in bed with a man and her no longer being worried about the couch, and I also said that becoming increasingly free from the more imperative and persecutory aspects of her prenatal longings was perhaps enabling her to enjoy their more helpful and non-persecutory aspects, as well as increasing her ability to use the more intuitive and "extra-sensory" (ESP) modes of foetal awareness, sensitivity, and communication.

In saying she could still not bear to think of her friend's death, Miss C had almost certainly given me yet another opportunity to understand that her dread of silences could indeed probably be explained by supposing that at one level, a "silent" me would probably be associated in her unconscious with a "dead" and dearly loved "friend"/me.

Session 10—7 days later—chair session

Miss C went straight to the chair, sat down, and told me with a smile that she did not "feel the need to come any more". Could she make this "the last session" and get in touch with me if she wanted to see me again? She said she could now tell her man friend when she did not "want to see him". She was no longer "possessive".

I pointed out the similarity between the two situations, the one with her man friend and the one with me, but she said she did not think they were "quite the same". With me it was more like wanting to "try [her] wings" and not "linger", and she gave me an instance of this not wanting to "linger". When she took her dog to prize shows, it often won a prize, in which case she always dashed off immediately after getting it. Prize-winners were expected to stay for a while after the end of the show so that people may have a chance of admiring the prize-winning dogs, but she always dashed off. She knew this "wasn't very nice", but it gave her a "terrific kick" to do it.

I again said that it seemed she was doing the same with me. She had won the "prize", the ability to enjoy sex, got "cured without getting too close", and now she wanted to go. She disagreed with this. It was more like "getting a bone healed and being able to walk again". (Had her friend's death "fractured" her spirit?)

Miss C then went on to say that it would be pointless to go on coming when there was nothing more to say. I asked if she still felt uneasy about silences. Her reply was: "No, it's not that there would be nothing I could say, it's just that there is nothing I want to say any more. At the beginning of seeing you, I wanted to claw something out, to disembowel someone. I felt something was sucking something out of me. Now I wouldn't want to hurt this man, he seems to be falling in love with me." I responded to this wish to "claw something out" or "disembowel someone" by interpreting it on Kleinian lines and as an expression of some remaining oral sadism; and I added that notwithstanding its possible prenatal connotations, her feeling of having something "sucked out" of her could also be explained by supposing that she had imagined a sucked-out "breast"/me as wanting to have its own back by doing the same to her (see again, in this connection, Segal, 1956, p. 340).

I had the uneasy feeling that in spite of her assertions to the contrary, her wish to stop coming was probably the re-enactment, in her relatedness to me, of what she had described as the "switching off" and the "pulling out" of a "plug", or perhaps the result of some remaining fear of silences, but I still couldn't see that unless she turned around to see me, my not talking would probably have caused her to experience me as dead.

It was obvious that she wanted to go, and I did not feel it right to ask her to stay just because there was something I did not understand.

She then said, with every sign of pleasure and gratitude but as if she was also rather puzzled and curious: "It has been a remarkably quick recovery, hasn't it?" I agreed, making no attempt to conceal the fact that I, too, was rather intrigued by this, and I asked her whether she had any ideas about what could have made it so "quick". She said it had all stemmed from the first session, when I had talked about the foetal nature of her vampire-like cravings and the resulting wish to be admitted to a prenatal mother/hospital. She said she had always known that her difficulties were "more than something sexual", "more than just an intense desire for a man or a woman's body", "even more than the craving of a baby for the mother". "Even that", she said—referring to the baby's insatiability—"didn't seem sufficient to explain the intensity of what I had felt".

I ventured the opinion that as early as the initial consultation, she had perhaps picked up signs of a special interest on my part in the prenatal stage, had experienced this as a special interest in her, and had begun to feel a little better as a result. She said she had not noticed any particular interest on my part in the prenatal phase or in her, but that she had thought quite a lot on her way home about what I had said, particularly about her wish to force her way back into her mother and her vampire-like greed being the remnant of the need for blood from the mother before birth. This had struck her as "something new", and it had "touched a chord". "It was the only thing", she said, "that had made sense of this need to claw something out, disembowel somebody" . . . "I used to feel that someone was sucking something away from me. I felt unbearable, and you were prepared to take on the burden." I said the word "burden" sounded like a baby. I then reminded her of the anxiety she had expressed, at the end of that first consultation, about whether, if admitted, she would be discovered to have "something horrible" inside her that would make her unbearable to other patients and cause her to be discharged; and I asked her whether my putting her name on the waiting list for admission could not have had a therapeutic effect in itself, by reassuring her that I did not see her as having something "unbearable" or "horrible" inside her that had to be kept away from people for their own sake. She agreed that knowing she could be admitted might have given her a feeling of security, but she again insisted that it was what I had said during the first session that had occupied her thoughts on the way home, the reason being that it had made "so much sense" to her. We had to finish on that note, for time was up. I wished her good luck, she said she was extremely grateful for the help she had received, and we parted. She did not contact me for a follow-up. I telephoned her family doctor a year or so later to find out how Miss C was faring and was told that she had gone abroad quite a while back and had left no forwarding address.

It later occurred to me that if one were to take the view that my interpreting my patient's "vampire" need of men on prenatal lines had in fact played a part in her "recovery", the latter could also have been helped by the fact that when talking to her face to face or from behind the couch, my voice, facial expression, and manner generally may have helped her to see that I had a fair degree of confidence in the possible usefulness of what I was saying. Such confidence may, therefore, have reassured Miss C that she was not so difficult to handle after all, or likely to have a bad effect on another human being (one of her other anxieties).

NOTES

1. See also Session 16, in which Miss A was to complain of the nurses trying to get rid of her by forming a "constricting" and "bearing-down" "circle" around her.

2. N. Symington has written about the possibility of regarding the therapist as sometimes becoming a "lassoed" victim of the patient's demands and expectations (1983, p. 287); see also below for what I thought, in the light of the next session (Session 16), to be Miss A's unconscious perception of me as a placental and umbilically tethered extension of her regressed and foetus-identified self.

3. At that stage, I did not yet know of DeMause's own work on the subject of prenatal symbolism and on placental symbolism in particular (1982, pp. 258–271).

4. This may be one way of looking at Bion's extremely useful concept of "attacks on linking" when dealing with patients who "attack" the interpretations offered to them (1959).

5. I have not checked this information for myself but was once given to understand that a 1953 WHO report had singled out a good "atmosphere" as perhaps the most important factor in a psychiatric hospital's ability to benefit people with psychological difficulties or disorders.

6. The situation in my old hospital is not the same now. When I used to work there, therapists were not expected to offer further help to a discharged patient in the form of outpatient follow-up. There was an outpatient department, but its facilities were hardly ever used by therapists for their discharged patients. Now that the outpatient department is being used for the follow-up of certain patients (Chiesa & Fonagy, 2003, p. 356), this could allow for the thought that at discharge (i.e. "birth"), and in the case of ex-inpatients who still show a certain degree of prenatal regression, the holding function of the erstwhile "prenatal mother"/hospital is taken over by the holding function of the analytic stance, with the interpretive work now acting as a placental link between the new "prenatal mother" therapist and the patient.

7. My decision to rather ruthlessly prune down an earlier and much longer draft of my report of Patient A's case has meant I have had to forgo what would otherwise have been an attempt to show and do justice to the way in which the reactions she had evoked in all of us, and particularly in the

nursing staff, during these last 48 hours of her first admission could also in retrospect be seen as having been played out at oral as well as oedipal levels of interaction.

8. I was later interested to see that G. Adler, writing this time with his analytic experience behind him and without any facetiousness, had himself found this idea of a "rebirth" quite useful to describe the successful working through of borderline regressive states (1974, p. 254); and that he had confirmed what he feels to have been the validity of the findings made in similar cases by such writers as Balint (1968), Guntrip (1971), Little (1960, 1966), Rosenfeld (1965), Winnicott (1965), and others.

9. In order to reduce the risk of prenatal regressions becoming harmful and too difficult to handle, the hospital in which the treatment of my Patient A had been carried out is now in favour of limiting the average length of stay to six months, followed by a period of approximately 18 months of outpatient follow-up in order to help the patient's re-adaptation to life in the outside world after the "birth" of discharge. When I used to work there, the average length of stay was around 9 months, and there was no outpatient follow-up. (For the present situation, see Chiesa & Fonagy, 2000, and, particularly, Chiesa & Fonagy, 2003, p. 356.

10. I am indebted to my colleague, the late Dr A. R. Wilson, for pointing out that "host" and "hospital" belong to the same family of words that include the word "hostile". This shared etymology is perhaps a good way of reminding ourselves of how easy it is for "hospitality" to turn into "hostility".

11. A year or so after the completion of her treatment, I tried to contact my patient to ask her whether she would allow me to use some of her material, but was told she had left the country without giving a forwarding address. If she comes across this book, I can only hope that she herself will take the view that the interest of her case made it worth publishing, and this despite the initial feeling of shock that reading my report may cause her.

12. See also Sidney Klein, 1980, p. 400, 1984, p. 313, and Laing, 1976, p. 58.

CHAPTER THREE

The placenta and its possible role in ego development

A few psychoanalytic writers have asked themselves whether it might be possible to conceive of a rudimentary "ego" that would operate even before birth (Fenichel, 1946, p. 34; Melanie Klein, 1952b, p. 263 n.; A. Rascovsky, 1956), and Hartmann suggested that "certain dispositions for future ego functions" may already be present "at birth (and actually before)" (1956, p. 250). The suggestion has even been made that an "unconscious ego-nucleus" ["*unbewusste Ich-Kern*"] might not only exist, but sometimes even suffer some damage during prenatal life, and that this could account for the difficulty in treating certain chronic tension states later (Ammon, 1974, p. 64). Should further psychoanalytic research confirm the usefulness of postulating the existence of a prenatal ego, the question may arise as to how such an "ego", at such an early stage, could best be conceived and represented.

The ego of classical psychoanalytic theory is usually, even if sometimes only tacitly, assumed to come into being at or soon after birth, and ever since Freud (1923b) it has been conceived as that part of the id's surface which from birth onwards increasingly differentiates itself from the id as a result of the latter's contact with the environment and becomes our main agent of communication with, and adaptation to, the world around us. It is also usually conceived (Hartmann, 1950) as a selective receptor of stimuli, an "inhibitor" of what it considers to be inappropriate impulses, an "organ" involved with such functions as "perception", "thinking", "mental self-regulation" (pp. 114–115), "adaptation", "synthesis", "organizing", and the "centralization of functional control" (p. 117). Hartmann was also interested (p. 117) in the feasibility of linking such properties with the findings of physiology and in the possibility of an eventual "meeting" of analytic ego[1] concepts with "physiological, especially brain-physiological, concepts"— presumably because he considered that some of the ego's functions just listed, if not all of them, were similar to those we normally associate with those of the brain, and that the latter could therefore be regarded as that part of the body most likely to act as one of the ego's main physical substrata and executive agents. Assuming the validity and usefulness of making this kind of link between ego function and brain function where postnatal life is concerned (postnatal life being almost certainly what Hartmann had here in mind), could the same kind of link be made with respect to intrauterine life? In other words, if we decided to postulate the existence of an ego operating as early as *in utero* and wanted to form some idea of what part of the unborn child could best be conceived as the main substructure, physical agent, or representative of this postulated prenatal ego, would it be legitimate here again to regard the brain—that is, the foetal brain—as the most likely contender for the role?

If the foetal brain could be shown to play a leading, controlling, and regulating part in the exchanges that take place between the unborn child and its "environment", this would presumably entitle us to regard it as fulfilling at least one of the functions we normally attribute to the ego, namely that of mediating between the individual and the outside world—the latter, in this case, being the inside of the mother's body and the mother as a person. The foetal brain, however, is relatively undeveloped and in far less direct contact with the maternal "environment" than is, say, the postnatal brain with respect to the external world. It is therefore difficult to see how its role in laying "certain dispositions for future ego functions", except perhaps in the later stages of the pregnancy, could be anything but rather limited. The foetal organ which is in most direct contact with the inside of the mother's body, which also plays the most active part in the unborn child's exchanges with its maternal "environment", is, of course, its placenta.[2] Without prejudice, therefore, to whatever role we think the foetal brain itself might play as a physical substructure to whatever we might decide to postulate as a foetal "ego", could an important part of this role be conceived as being also carried out by the foetus' placenta? My reasons for thinking that it could perhaps be so conceived are set out below. I apologize for the repetition but could see no way of avoiding it.

1. As mentioned earlier, Freud saw the ego as originating from that part of the id's surface which differentiated itself from the id's surface as a result of its contact with the environment and became our main agent of communication with, and adaptation to, the world around us. In somewhat similar fashion, the foetal part of the placenta evolves from the development and differentiation of that part of the fertilized egg's surface which is in contact at the embryonic pole with the maternal tissues during its implantation into the endometrium and which, in the fully formed placenta, will not only be "an area of contact between the egg and the maternal tissues for the purposes of physiological exchange" (after Davies, 1963, p. 17) but also constitute what could likewise be regarded as an organ of communication with, and adaptation to, the growing embryo and its maternal environment.

2. Freud wrote about the way in which the ego not only seeks and takes in objects from the external world, but also "expels" into it whatever it needs to reject (1915c, pp. 135–136). The placenta can be regarded as an organ of the foetus by means of which the latter not only extracts from the mother's blood the oxygen and nutrients it needs in order to survive, but also expels into this blood what it needs to reject (CO_2, urea, etc.).

3. Hartmann described the ego as an "organ" of "centralized functional control" (1956, p. 291), which organized and synthesized such functions as "adaptation", "control" and "integration" (p. 290). He also referred to it as a "biological agent" (p. 291). The placenta, too, is a biological agent, and it, too, can be said to "centralize", in one single "organ", "functions" that will be distributed at birth to other organs such as the lungs (respiratory

function), the digestive tract (nutritive function), and the excretory system (the placenta's detoxifying function).

4. In keeping with Freud, Hartmann saw the ego as a "protective barrier" against excessive stimuli (1950, p. 115), and Fenichel had written about the way in which it proceeded "selectively in its reception of stimuli" (1946, p. 16). The thin placental membrane or "barrier", often referred to as a "selective barrier", "protects" the foetus against possible immunological clashes with the mother by keeping their respective bloods separate, and it, too, proceeds "selectively" in the exchanges of gases and nutrients that take place between the two (Page, 1963, p. 147).

5. Hartmann mentioned the role that the ego plays in "thinking", and in acting as an organ of "mental self-regulation" (1950, p. 115). Research into placental function has suggested that the concentration of materials on either side of the placental membrane cannot be explained by a mere process of diffusion operating according to the simple laws of physics, and that the endothelial and syncytial cells that constitute the thin placental membrane can, therefore, be deemed to play an active part in controlling and regulating the rate at which these exchanges take place (Page, 1963). It would thus seem possible: (a) to conceive of the self-regulation performed by the placenta (and more specifically by the so-called placental membrane), as one of the main physical forerunners of the mental forms of self-regulation that will be increasingly performed after birth by the rapidly developing ego or "brain-ego"; and (b) to regard this self-regulation as the beginning of the kind of "intelligence" that Bion suggested could be already at work in the foetus or even in the embryo (1980, p. 22). Another possible reason for regarding the placenta as performing the function of some self-regulating and prenatal kind of ego could be the role that some authors have suggested the placenta could play, by means of a sudden drop in oestrogen secretion, in determining the onset of labour (Langman, 1969, p. 78).

6. Finally, the placenta could be described as a mirror that "reflects" to the foetus what one hopes will be a good image of itself ("good" oxygen and nutrients in exchange for "bad" foetal wastes), and since psychoanalytical theory has always

regarded "thinking" and "reflecting" as an essentially "ego" kind of function, it might not be too far-fetched to regard the ego's ability to "reflect"—that is, to send back to oneself thoughts one has had and can then consider at leisure—as the evolutionary continuation and perfecting of the placenta's own "reflexive function".[3]

The question I am therefore raising here is the following. In view of the parallel it would seem possible to draw between what biology can tell us about the origin and functions of the placenta on the one hand and what classical psychoanalytical theory considers to be those of the ego on the other, would it be possible to think in terms of some form of continuity between the two: to conceive for example, the postnatal ego as so to speak taking over, at birth and in mental form, some of the functions that the placenta had previously carried out in physiological form between the unborn child and its maternal environment? By the same token, and provided we were prepared to accept Hartmann's idea of a close identity of functions between brain and ego, could we perhaps also conceive of a "brain" sort of "ego" as taking over, after birth, the role that the placenta had carried out before birth by "synthesizing" various functions and by acting, not only as an organ of "centralized functional control", but also as our main agent of communication with the environment?

I am not, of course, suggesting that the brain or postnatal "brain-ego" is the only organ that could be conceived as continuing in postnatal life some of the functions that had been carried out in prenatal life by the placenta. At birth the postnatal lungs can be said to take over the placenta's "respiratory" function and to become a kind of internalized, respiratory, postnatal "placenta"; the greater part of the digestive tract takes over the placenta's function as a supplier of nutrients; and the kidneys, together with the end of the digestive tract, take over the placenta's function as an eliminator of foetal wastes. On the other hand, the postnatal brain increasingly acts as a kind of "overlord" to all these functions and can thus be regarded as having under its control a number of subsidiary organs or "egos". E. Glover (1943) had already suggested the possibility of conceiving the postnatal ego as the end result of the gradual fusion and integration of a number of "nuclear" egos that arise, immediately after birth, "from different body zones and organ centres" (pp. 10–12). This concept of an initial "multi-nuclear ego" (p. 10) is, of course, reminiscent of what embryology tells us about the way in which the embryo itself results from the gradual and eventual fusion of and integration between a number of "different body zones and organ centres", to borrow from Glover's words.

It may also be worth mentioning here that authors who have studied the possible prenatal forerunners or even determinants of postnatal behaviour from a psychiatric and physiological point of view have shown that foetal malnutrition due to placental disease or malfunction can cause structural and biochemical changes in the brain and that these, if not compensated for by good neonatal care, may be responsible for mental impairment and behavioural disorders in later life (Winick, 1983). These findings were obtained by following up the development of children who were known to have suffered from placental impairment. Psychoanalysts interested in this kind of research will presumably prefer to work in reverse by trying to see whether, in addition to other possible contributory factors, patients who have shown signs of severe ego impairment can sometimes later be found to have a placental history and whether, within certain limits that I shall shortly define, some degree of correlation can be established between the former and the latter.

It is not easy to measure the "severity" of ego-impairment, but for the purposes of the proposed inquiry it would seem logical to assume that one of the markers that could make us suspect the presence, and also assess the extent, of some ego defect could be the number of occasions when the patient's analyst or analytically oriented therapist had felt it necessary to deviate from his mainly interpretive stance and to adopt, in order to help his patient over a crisis, the more managerial role of becoming for the latter a kind of "auxiliary" ego. There is admittedly a certain disadvantage in making a patient's ability to induce this change of stance one of the criteria of "severe ego impairment", since some analysts or therapists may deem it justified to take on the role of auxiliary ego in cases where others would have considered the crisis quite capable of being handled by interpretive means only. Even so, and as long as one is aware that any therapeutic intervention, be it interpretive or managerial, is never completely free from the influence of personal factors in the therapist, whether one likes it or not, the ability of a patient to make the analyst or therapist take on the role of auxiliary ego may be as good a criterion as any by which to assess the strength, weakness, or soundness of his patient's ego.

Perhaps I can mention here what I thought may have been two instances of my intervening as a kind of auxiliary "placental ego". Patient A (chapter two) had made what could have been a serious suicide attempt as an almost immediate response to her nurse's inability to attend to her as promptly as she, the patient, must have hoped she would. The nursing staff had expressed grave concern about being expected to be responsible for such an unpredictable and impulsive patient during nights and weekends when the duty doctor was only on call at the end of a telephone. This had made me deem it safer to arrange for my patient to be transferred back to the psychiatric hospital that had referred her to us for psychotherapy, and the team had agreed. On my telling the patient this, she had produced new material that had made me see what we were about to act out. Encouraged by what I thought to be this new insight into the situation, I had tried to obtain a postponement of the patient's discharge, but this had not been successful.

At a postnatal level, it had been possible in retrospect to see my intervening for my patient in this way as a piece of countertransference acting out in which I had stepped into the role of a supportive but somewhat ineffectual mother. Subsequent material, however, had made me realize, belatedly, that when looking at things from a pre- and perinatal point of view, I could also be said to have unwittingly acted out a placental sort of role in order to try to help my patient maintain her adhesion to the uterine wall of a phantasied "prenatal mother"/hospital that was showing signs of no longer being able or willing to hold her. Much later still, when I became interested in the possibility of making some kind of comparison between placental and ego functions, I realized that in acting out this "placental" sort of role, I could also be said to have taken on that of an auxiliary kind of ego and to have done this because of some instinctive and unconscious realization that my patient was too disturbed at that point to have been able to use her wits to plead her own case by herself—not that I had done a very good job of this myself as my proposal of an extension of stay had not been accepted by the team.

On her repeated pleas to be given a second chance, however, my patient had been readmitted, and the second instance in which I thought I could be said to have acted as a placental-cum-auxiliary ego for her had occurred in the course of this second admission. On the eve of a fairly prolonged Christmas break and in response to her having once again made me sufficiently anxious about the possibility of another suicidal acting out, I had asked her if it would help for me to have a word with the nursing staff, whom I knew she might be reluctant to approach herself. She had agreed, and I later realized that there again, and without my realizing this at the time, I may have offered myself as some kind of placental go-between to make her less tempted, during my absence, to sever her connection with the "body" of a once again phantasied "prenatal mother"/hospital.

A delinquent youth, whom I was seeing in my capacity of visiting psychiatrist at the penal institution where he was serving a sentence, surprised me one day by producing what seemed to be a spontaneous association between the placenta and the head and thus, by implication, between the placenta and the postulated brain-ego. He had several times tried to make me play the role of some kind of go-between by asking me if I could tell him what the prison officers were saying about him, or if I could speak to them on his behalf so that he could obtain some favour that he was afraid or reluctant to ask of them himself. He also seemed bent on trying to make me say that what he felt or thought about some issue or other was fully justified, so that he could have me on his side or as someone whose opinion he could then oppose to whichever staff member might disagree with him. Further questioning revealed that his parents had often disagreed and quarrelled about various matters or decisions and the boy often used one parent to support his case against the other, and that when he wanted some favour that he knew his father would refuse if he approached the latter direct, he would ask his mother to speak to him on his behalf. Not unexpectedly in a boy who had been in trouble with the law several times already, my telling him that he was now repeating some of his behaviour in his relationship to the staff and me had no visible effect, and his demands on me continued.

Previous material, the exact nature of which I can no longer recall, had already caused me to ask him whether he knew anything about the circumstances of his birth, and this had made him remember his mother once saying that the labour had been long and painful. I therefore decided to try to see whether I could find anything to support the idea that the ordeal he may have gone through as a result of a difficult birth could have made it difficult for him to transfer to his postnatal mind and brain the linking, "thinking", mediating, and "decision-making" functions that his placenta had conceivably carried out for him in prenatal life,[4] and whether this postulated and difficult "handover" of functions could, therefore, be one of the reasons for his repeated attempts to get me to assume these functions for him.

I therefore told him that his requests for me to act as a go-between for him in his dealings with the staff, and as some kind of decision-making or back-up agency for his thinking, had given me an idea that I wanted to put to the test, but that as this would involve my referring to the way in which the unborn child communicated with the pregnant mother, I first wanted to make sure that he had at least some idea of how this communication took place so that he could better understand what I was about to say. Did he know, for example, what was meant by the word "placenta"? He said he thought it had something to do with the cord. I therefore proceeded to explain. I had just started to say that the placenta was an external organ of the foetus, attached to the latter by the umbilical cord, when he brightly stopped me to ask: "You mean like the 'ead"? (the "head" for readers unfamiliar with London cockney accents). Thinking of the obvious association one can make between the "brain-ego" and the "head", I asked him what had suddenly made him think of the head.

He said he had never seen the head as something that was part of the body. The body was everything below the neck. The head was simply something else, which was attached to the body by the neck; and he confirmed that this was why he had thought of the head when I had spoken about the placenta being attached to the foetus by the umbilical cord. His transfer to another unit shortly after this gave me no opportunity to follow him up, but I could not help being intrigued by this youngster's apparently spontaneous rejoinder, especially since I had never, in that particular institution at any rate, said anything about my particular interests, nor ever noticed any ability on my part to communicate my thought to my fellow human beings by means of telepathy.

Further references to the literature that could be made here are the following: The idea that there might be a link in the unconscious between the placenta and the brain, particularly the cortical brain, had already been put forward by Mott as a result of his extensive research into dream symbolism (1964, p. 735). Blomfield (1985) had seen the placenta as that part of the foetus by which the latter exercises, in its relatedness to the host-mother, the ruthlessness of its "parasitic intentionality" (p. 305)—a view that makes me wonder whether Blomfield might have been prepared to accept the idea of a foetal and possibly placental kind of "ego" the "intentionality" of which would be at the root of all "human destructiveness" (see also Blomfield, 1987). When writing about the "perturbances of symbiosis and individuation of the psychotic ego" (the title of her paper), Mahler expressed the view that "the core disturbance in infantile psychosis is a deficiency or a defect in the child's ability to utilize the "good" mothering agency as distinct from the self" (1971, p. 191).[5] As far as I can tell, Mahler made no specific mention of the part that placental disease or malfunction can play in affecting the unborn child's ability to "utilize" a prenatal and averagely "good" mothering agency, but she would no doubt have taken that possibility for granted.

Tustin's work with autistic children can itself be said to offer a wealth of opportunities for furthering our understanding of ego formation and impairment. I was particularly interested in her observations (1981, p. 97) that autistic children appear to be suffering from the loss, not only of an "object", but of a part of their body. As Laing has suggested (1976, p. 58), the loss of the placenta at birth may not always be easily or completely overcome. Again. as far as I can tell, Tustin has not expressed any view as to whether autistic children who appear to have lost a part of their "body" could have failed to overcome the loss of the placental part of their former prenatal self or "body", but although I have no experience of working with children, I have sometimes asked myself if some research along those lines might be worth undertaking—including, of course, some research into whether autistic children may have suffered from some defective communication with their mother even before birth. As I later realized (see Maiello, 1997, p. 89), Tustin herself had envisaged that possibility and so, incidentally, has Maiello herself (2001). All I am adding here is that deprivation or trauma occurring *in utero* can sometimes result from some degree of placental defect, malfunction, or injury.

In a paper on narcissism and projective identification, Sohn (1985) proposed the term "the identificate" to refer to that split-off part of the ego which is "projected" into the object. By this term he underlined the "concretely differentiated" nature of the split-off part (p. 205), its relative autonomy, and its power of "omnipotent control" (p. 205). Could the "identificate" represent the postnatal and psychological continuation of the placenta—that is, that quasi "split-off" part of the prenatal self which the latter "projects" into the maternal "object" and which could also be said to exert some kind of "omnipotent control" over her, regulating as it does so much of the exchange that take place between the mother and the foetal body proper?

Finally, I can perhaps make another mention of the fact that the main "object" of the prenatal drive is presented in certain writings as the "placenta" (Sidney Klein, 1980, p. 400, 1984, p. 313; Paul, 1983, p. 561); whereas in other writings (Grunberger, 1983, pp. 925–926, and probably also Blomfield, 1985, 1987) it has been referred to as the mother herself. This has made me wonder whether it might in fact be useful to postulate the existence of two types of prenatal transference: one in which the patient would be deemed to have retained some ability to use what I called his "brain-ego" (regressed though it may be to a more primitive and "placental" type of functioning) as a "placental" sort of link between himself and the therapist/"mother"; and another, more "placental" type of prenatal transference in which he would have handed over this "placental" function to the therapist and expect the latter to act as this "thinking", "linking", and "reflecting" sort of object himself: something that would then presumably amount to the patient's almost complete inability or unwillingness to think and "reflect" for himself.[6]

Returning now to the main theme of the present chapter, if there is some justification for postulating some kind of "handover", at birth, of the physiologically discriminating and "reflecting"[7] function of the placenta to the newborn's rapidly developing "brain" or "brain-ego", a patient's inability or unwillingness to reflect and cooperate would presumably justify speculating about what could have caused such a "handover" to have gone wrong for one reason or another: a degree of placental defect or malfunction, a traumatic birth, inadequate postnatal care, or a combination of all three?

As the reader must have grown tried of my speculations long before now, I had better conclude. I am aware that this chapter too has done nothing but ask a few questions, and I am sure it has also shown how difficult it is to know whether they are useful questions to ask in the first place. In the 32nd of his *New Introductory Lectures*, Freud remarked that "the findings of psychology take us to the frontiers of biological fact" (1933a, p. 115). I do not know whether psychology will one day be able to cross that frontier, but it would seem a pity if it did not at least explore the possibility of doing so. Meanwhile, one cannot but agree with Eisenberg when, referring to a 1983 paper by Hahn and Kleinman, he wrote about the "daunting" task of trying to understand "the ways in which the mind is embodied and the body literally mindful" (Eisenberg, 1986, p. 505).

NOTES

1. Yorke (1994, p. 376 n.) has drawn attention to the fact that Freud "sometimes used "ego" to refer to the "self" and at other times to denote the "executive apparatus of the mind." It will be obvious from what I say in this chapter that I am using the second of these two definitions, which, as Yorke also points out, has been generally accepted by most analysts since the publication of *The Ego and the Id* in 1923. If Yorke is right in adding that "with rare exceptions" Melanie Klein always used the term "ego" "to mean the self" and that this was "the sense followed by almost all her associates and successors", my referring to it here as the self's executive organ could be regarded as a minor departure from Kleinian terminology or even thinking. On the other hand, my associating myself with those writers who have speculated about the possible existence and interpretability of prenatal levels of transference (Blomfield, 1985, 1987; Sidney Klein, 1980, p. 400, 1984, p. 313; Paul, 1983, p. 561; A. & M. Rascovsky, 1971a, pp. 28–29; A. Rascovsky et al., 1971b; Simmel, 1929, pp.

86–87; N. Symington, 1981, p. 195), as well as with those who have even suggested the possible usefulness of conceiving of a prenatal form of aggressivity (Blomfield, 1985, 1987; Grunberger, 1983, pp. 925–926, 935; A. Rascovsky, 1956, p. 289; Verny, 1981, p. 84), may not be seen to amount to anything more than proposing a logical and almost built-in extension of existing Kleinian theory.

2. I say "its" placenta because although, as mentioned earlier, the placenta is a hybrid organ the formation and development of which is contributed to by both foetus and mother, the fact that the greater part of its structure is derived from the egg and that its most actively functional part, the placental membrane, is "composed exclusively of foetal tissue" (Langman, 1969, p. 77) allows one to regard it as a mainly foetal organ and the one by means of which the unborn child relates to the mother's body.

3. In a privately circulated paper, Pines (1992) likens the inability to "reflect" (in the mental sense of the word) to a defective kind of "mirroring" (p. 21), and he then goes on to refer to the "biological mirroring" that takes place between the infant and its mother in the form of the repeated exchange of visual, auditory, and tactile stimuli between the two members of the couple (p. 24). In that paper, Pines pays special attention to the important role played by auditory stimuli and the mother's voice in particular, and to the way in which listening and being listened to make such an important contribution to the development of our sense of being "human". Some allusion to a prenatal and amniotic kind of "reflecting" was also suggested to me by Pines' repeated reference to the early experience of being "immersed in a bath of sound" (p. 25); and when he writes, a little earlier on that same page, that we are "immersed in a sonorous world in *uterine* (emphasis added) and postnatal life onwards", this seemed to me to express his own interest in the possible existence of a "biological mirroring" that could take place as early as *in utero* and perhaps influence postnatal reactions to the environment (see also Maiello, 1995).

4. By the words "thinking" and "decision making" I am once again referring to what appears to be the active role played by the endothelial cells of the foetal capillaries that bathe in the maternal blood of the placental blood lakes, in regulating the exchange that takes place between the two bloods, and in therefore "deciding" what should pass from one to the other in either direction at any one moment (Page, 1963, p. 147).

5. I cannot associate myself entirely with Mahler's view that it is "physiology rather than psychology" that will "show us the way to decipher the enigma of psychosis". I think physiology will help, but even though unfortunately my work has not brought me into contact with patients suffering from truly psychotic forms of disorders, it must be obvious that, as far as treatment is concerned, my main interest would lie in the psychological approach pioneered by Bion (1953, 1956, 1957), Grotstein (1977a, 1977b), Meltzer (1963a, 1963b, 1974, 1975), Rosenfeld (1947, 1950, 1952a, 1952b, 1971); Searles (1965), Segal (1950, 1956, 1981), Sohn (1985), and others.

6. I should perhaps point out here that the terms "placental transference" and "prenatal mother transference" are being used here to denote what would then be regarded, in each of the two hypothetical types or levels of prenatal transference, as the transference's main object. When we use the terms "oral", "anal", "genital", and so on to refer to postnatal levels of transference, these

terms indicate not what is deemed to be the main "object" of the transference concerned but, rather, the developmental stage or level that they seem to be enacting. I am not sure why, but it somehow seems easier to define the two postulated prenatal levels of transference according to whichever would seem to be their main "object"—that is, the placental (but now discarded or disowned part of the patient's prenatally regressed self), or the phantasied "prenatal mother"/therapist.

7. Cf. my earlier remarks about the placenta as a kind of physiological "mirror", and of this function being possibly the beginning of what will later become the ability to "reflect" in the mental sense of the word.

CHAPTER FOUR

Notes on placental symbolism

Almost from the moment when psychoanalysis started to take shape as a therapeutic procedure, the possibility that the womb, the umbilical cord, and intra-uterine life generally, could sometimes be alluded to in patients' material by means of the appropriate symbols seems to have been taken almost for granted in the writings of most analysts; but the possibility that the placenta, too, could sometimes be alluded to or communicated about by means of objects susceptible of evoking its configuration, structure, and functions does not seem even now to have received the kind of attention accorded to the symbologenicity of, say, the womb or the umbilical cord. Is the loss at birth of that part of our erstwhile prenatal self that has enabled us to live off the mother's body before birth more difficult to think about than the loss of the mother herself?

The earliest reference to the possible existence of placental symbols seems to have been made by Lietaert Peerbolte in a paper published in the *Psychoanalytic Quarterly* in 1951. Roheim mentioned the placenta in his book *The Gates of the Dream* (1952, p. 483), but more from an anthropological point of view than a psychoanalytic one. Mott gave several instances of what he thought to be placental symbols, both in his book on mythology (1960, pp. 6, 54–56) and in his extensive study of dreams (1964, pp. 309–316, 692–693, 727–729, 788).

I mentioned what I, too, thought might be placental symbols in a short paper (Ployé, 1973), and I list a few more "possibles" later in this chapter. R. D. Laing, much influenced by Mott, showed his interest in the subject in a small book published in 1976. An extremely detailed and useful study of suggested placental symbols can be found in the last chapter of Lloyd DeMause's book *Foundations of Psychohistory* (1982), but I have not yet been able to ascertain whether references to the placenta had already appeared in other works by him. Dowling (1988, pp. 535–540) wrote an interesting article about the possible placental symbolism of the "tree" and the way he felt it could be put to use in therapy. He also mentioned (p. 536) what seemed to him to have been possible but unwitting allusions to the placenta in some of the writings that Jung had collected from alchemists concerning the symbolism of the "tree". In her doctoral dissertation on "Birth and Infant Trauma", which contained many references to prenatal life (1992), and in her later book on the reconstruction of infant and prenatal trauma (1994), Share mentioned the reference I made to possible placental symbolism in my 1973 paper; but my research of the literature has not been as thorough as it should have been, and although the above references to the possible existence of placental symbols are the only ones I have so far been able to find among the several writings that have appeared concerning the possible relevance of prenatal life to postnatal psychology, there may be others I have not yet come across.

The only explicit instances I have been able to find of the placenta being mentioned as a possible transference object are papers by Sidney Klein (1980, p. 400, 1984, p. 313) and by Paul (1983, p. 561). Blomfield (1985, 1987) saw the placenta less as the "object" of the foetus' needs and cravings than as the instrument or agent by means of which the foetus exercises its parasitic aggressivity against what can then be conceived as the main "object" of the foetal drive, namely the prenatal mother herself.

I suggested earlier in this book that when looking at things from a prenatal point of view, the holding and containing aspect of the analytic stance can be conceived as continuing the role that the womb and the prenatal mother have played in holding and containing the unborn child, and that the therapist's interpretive function can be conceived as carrying out, between the prenatal levels of the patient's self and the maternal holding of the analytic stance, a role not unlike the linking and discriminating function that the patient's placenta had played in mediating between him and his or her mother in prenatal life. Research into such matters, if undertaken, could be made easier by assuming the existence of placental symbols and, if such appeared in the material, by trying to see whether the surrounding context might make possible a reconstruction of prenatal events. The connection between known cases of placental defect or disease and the appearance of psychiatric forms of disorder in life after birth has already been established (Winick, 1983), but analysts or psychoanalytically oriented therapists could explore such connections for themselves with their own particular skills and methods.

The suggestion is therefore put forward that it might be useful to form some idea of the sort of objects, metaphors, turns of phrase, and so on, that the unconscious could logically be expected to use to represent and communicate about the placenta if such symbolism exists.

Several of the symbols listed below have been mentioned already by some of the authors mentioned above, but I have added some more. I have not been able to test any of them clinically because I no longer practise; I have simply used a little of what Bion referred to as "speculative imagination" (1980, p. 27). As Freud said: "The field of symbolism is immensely wide, and dream symbolism is only a part of it" (1916–17, p. 166).

List of suggested placental symbols

1. Although not exactly a "symbol", a possible placental "marker" could be the patient's unconscious expectation that the therapist be prepared to act as a mere extension of the patient's own self, thoughts, and feelings, or as a pleasant, unobtrusive, "alter-ego"-like companion in the security of a womb-like consulting-room; or again, and, in the more severe type of cases,

as a mediating, discriminating sort of filter as well as communicating agent between the patient and other people (such as seemed to have been the case in patient A, whose material is reported in chapter two).

2. An *"open parachute"*: same configuration, life-preserving function (see Mott, 1964, p. 788).
3. A *"flying kite"*: flying a kite = sending a probe to explore the reactions of other people. The foetus reaches for the "beyond" of the mother's body, and of the world she herself lives in, by its umbilical cord and placenta.
4. An *"open umbrella"*: configuration and protective function.
5. *"Luggage"*: many people dream of luggage that they have left behind, and which they frantically go back for and can never find; the placenta as a part of ourselves that is left behind at birth, and the loss of which we may not always be able to make up for.
6. An *"anchor"*: symbol of security and attachment; the womb as the harbour.
7. A *"grappling iron"*: the placenta as something that makes sure we do not fall off the uterine wall.
8. A *"ball and chain"*: symbol of the more persecutory aspects of prenatal attachment; the placental "ball" at the end of the umbilical "chain".
9. A *"spider's web"*: the web or mesh of umbilical capillaries inside the placenta. Reversibility of this proposed symbolism. The spider as the foetus, casting its web inside the woman (the latter's fear of getting pregnant); or the spider as the woman herself, in whose web the male is afraid of getting caught.
10. A *"cake"*: placenta = Latin equivalent of the Greek word *"plakounta"*, which is the accusative of *"plakous:"* a flat cake; a "sponge cake" (spongious consistency of the placenta); "sponging" on people, the State, and so on; a "birthday cake" (birth, candles as placental villi, symbol of life). Is a person who wants to have his (or her) cake "and eat it" still looking for the placental "cake" from which, as an unborn child, he or she had been able to "feed" without ceasing to have it? The "reality" of

the inexhaustible placenta as a forerunner of the "phantasy" of the inexhaustible breast?

11. A *"sponge"*: see above; parasitism ("sponging").

12. A *"wheel"*: circular shape, spokes of the wheel as the foetal blood vessels radiating from the point of insertion of the umbilical cord—that is, from the "hub" of the placental "wheel".

13. A *"spinning top"*: circular shape, hollowness, the placenta as a hollow disc.

14. A *"flying saucer"*: same as above: a mysterious object from another world, the "prenatal" world.

15. A *"tree"*: the umbilical cord as the trunk, the branches, and foliage as the ramification of umbilical capillaries that spread into the "atmosphere" of the maternal blood, from which they get their oxygen, just as leaves get their CO2 from the surrounding air. The image can be reversed (the umbilical capillaries as the roots that spread into the soil [blood] of the mother [earth]; see Dowling, 1988).

16. *"Aquatic ferns"* rising from the river bed: same image as above; the umbilical capillaries that sprout inside the maternal blood inside the placenta.

17. Certain types of *"mushrooms"*, particularly the ones with a flat or rounded top: when looked at from underneath, they again resemble the foetal face of the placenta, with vessels radiating from the centre. Mushrooms can also be poisonous. Possible allusion to those moments when the placenta, if foetal wastes are not evacuated quickly enough (or if the mother smokes, drinks, or takes drugs), could itself become "poisonous".

18. The *"lotus flower"*: the Buddha sits on it and merges with the "One" or the Universal "self"; Nirvana—so-called "blissful union with the mother's womb".

19. The *"moon"*: a round disc in the sky that brings light (survival) in the "darkness" of the womb. A disc of which we only ever see one side, just as the foetus always faces the foetal face of the placental "disc". The moon as a possible placental symbol was first mentioned by Lietaert Peerbolte (1951, pp. 598–599, 1975, p. 9). In his book "The Gates of the Dream", Roheim quotes

from *Malekula: A Vanishing People in the New Hebrides* by A. B. Deacon and says: "In the New Hebrides according to Seniang tradition, the moon is closely associated with childbirth. The marks on the surface of the moon are the afterbirth, and at the first full moon after delivery the people will point to it and say: 'Look, there is the placenta'" (Roheim, 1952, p. 483).

20. *"Janus"*, the Roman God of "doors", usually depicted as having two faces, one that looks inside the house and one that looks outside: the two "faces" of the placenta, one turned towards the foetus and the other towards the mother, the "outside" (prenatal) world. This image, too, can be reversed: the inside of the mother as the first "house" we live in, so that in that case one "face" of the placenta is turned towards the inside of the house and the other towards the exit—that is, the "door" from which the unborn child will leave the "house" at birth. Janus, the God of all doorways through which all things pass, back and forth; the exchanges that take place between mother and foetus, back and forth through the placental membrane. In a pejorative sense, a "two-faced" person, "running with the hare and chasing with the hounds"; in a "good" sense: a "mediator", a "communicator", a "janitor", keeper of the "door". A mention of a possible case of "placenta praevia" was made in an earlier work (Ployé, 1973, p. 244), but anamnestic confirmation could not be obtained.

21. A *"mirror"*: the placenta, fixed on the uterine "wall", "reflects" to the foetus the blood that the latter projects on or into it via the two umbilical arteries. The blood returns to the foetus via the umbilical vein, and since it is relatively free of waste compared to what it was when leaving the foetus, it could be said to "reflect" to the latter an improved "image" of itself. Narcissus, Death. Foetal regression as something that is sometimes necessary and healing, as in sleep; just as a certain amount of "self-love" is a condition of mental health; but also the opposite of this: foetal regression and excessive self-love as death: absorbed in the contemplation of his own image in the placental "mirror" (the "pond"), Narcissus eventually dies. Also, since in postnatal life the mother's face is sometimes described as a "mirror" that helps the infant by not normally sending back to

it a hateful image of itself when it projects onto it all its screams, distress, or hate: could the mother's face also continue, in early postnatal life, and indeed throughout life itself (the "face" of the beloved), a placental sort of function?

22. A *"protective shield"*: the placenta as a shield that protects the foetus, not only against any backflow of the wastes that the latter has emptied into it (and from there into the mother's bloodstream), but also, by means of the placental "barrier" that prevents the two bloods from mixing, against the immunological clashes that would otherwise take place between the two. It is, however, worth pointing out that the placenta is by no means as reliable a protective shield against mother-inflicted noxae—like nicotine, alcohol, drugs, and so on—as one fondly imagined it to be in the past.

23. Any reference to a *selective "grid"* or *"barrier"*: a *"filter"*, a *"sieve"*: possible allusion to the placenta membrane, often referred to as a "selective barrier".

24. References to a *"go-between"*, *"middle-man"*, *"mediator"*, *"pig-in-the-middle"*: self-evident, but also see No. 20, and references to a "double-agent".

25. An *"octopus"*: frightening object lurking in dark waters that could be particularly frightening to underwater divers if, apart from latching onto a part of their body, it also had a rock to hold on to with some of its other tentacles, thus preventing the diver from getting back to the surface. The placenta as adhering to the uterine "wall"; "adhesive" quality of certain transferences; "tentacles" as the spread of the foetal capillaries. As in the case of the "spider" (No. 9), reversibility of the symbol: the octopus as the foetus that clings and adheres to the uterine wall of the pregnant mother; or as the woman herself, in whose "tentacles" the male is afraid of getting caught. My own feeling is that these frightening images of the mother can be contributed to by the patient's projection of his own unconscious parasitism and the resulting fear of retaliation—not a new idea, simply an extension and reformulation of the Kleinian notion of the retaliatory breast or "inside of the mother's body". On the other hand, there could of course be cases where the inside of the mother's body had actually been a dangerous place to be in and where

the said images could then be the result of what Melanie Klein had referred to as "unpleasant experiences *in utero*" (1957, p. 492).

26. A *"limpet"*, *"barnacles"*, etc.: adhesion to the uterine wall, "adhesive" forms of identification.

27. The *"Giant"* in the "Jack and the Beanstalk" story: the giant pursues the boy, who escapes by quickly sliding down the beanstalk back to mother and by cutting the stalk down as soon as the giant has started his own descent. Birth, and the cutting of the umbilical "stalk" as an escape from what would otherwise be a dangerous placenta, rendered dangerous because of its having become fibrous and no longer able to sustain life. During the pregnancy itself, the same umbilical cord could be the stalk that the foetus climbs in order to obtain the "treasures" of the "castle" (inside of the mother's body), with the sympathetic complicity of the giant's wife, the "good" prenatal mother. This tale is also a possible example of the frequent blending of oedipal (genital) and prenatal symbolism, and of the interchangeability between penis and umbilical cord symbols (compare Chasseguet-Smirgel's proposals concerning the possible existence of prenatal origins or "matrix" of the Oedipus complex, 1984b, 1992).

28. A *"danger coming from the sky"*: "bombs", "pollution" of the air: the placenta possibly experienced as a threat in cases of placental disease or defect, or when an otherwise healthy placenta is unable to cope with, say, maternal toxaemia, drugs, or other noxae contained in the mother's blood.

29. Following on from this theme of air "pollution" or "danger coming from the sky" and returning to the "tree" as a possible placental symbol (No.15, above), could there have been a placental underscoring to the dream that Freud's "Wolf Man" patient had had as a child—that is, that in which the latter had dreamt of seeing, just outside his bedroom window, which had suddenly opened of its own accord, a large walnut tree on the various branches of which six or seven white wolves were silently sitting, staring at him fixedly (Freud, 1918b, p. 29).

The patient's associations to the "white wolves" when recalling this dream in his analysis as an adult had been to some white sheep that had, in reality, died as a result of a severe infection in spite of their having been inoculated against it (pp. 30–34). One of his associations to the "tree" and the wolves on its branches had been to a Christmas tree charged with presents (pp. 35–36), and he had been born on Christmas day (pp. 15, 35).

A chain of further associations, which need not be mentioned here, had caused Freud to speculate about the possibility that his patient may, as a very young child, have witnessed the so-called "primal scene" and seen his naked parents making love (pp. 36–39). But could one raise two additional questions?

a. At early postnatal level, could the white wolves have also stood for white breasts that had originally been experienced as good (good and welcome Christmas or birthday "presents"), but later turned bad (the infected white sheep)?

b. At pre/or perinatal level, could the "tree" have represented an unconsciously remembered "placenta/tree" that had likewise been originally experienced as good—that is, charged with the "presents" of "good" oxygen and nutrients—and later also turned "bad" as a result of its blood becoming contaminated—that is, "infected" like the sheep—by an excess of foetal wastes such as Co^2 or urea?[1] In addition to my thinking here of the interest which Melanie Klein was beginning to show towards the end of her life in the possibility of conceiving of "bad" as well as "good" prenatal experiences (1957, p. 179), I am also struck by the fact that the "Wolf Man" appears to have treated the analytic setting as a kind of womb in which he felt comfortably "entrenched" (Freud, 1918b, p. 11); that in order to bring the treatment to an end, Freud had had to resort to fixing a date for its termination—like in some sort of "induction of labour" (p. 11); and that the patient's "womb phantasies", which Freud mentioned at the end of his paper, had seemed real enough.

30. Could certain cases of *"folie à deux"* be a kind of prenatal regression in which two people, locked in a commonly shared "womb" of phantasy and delusion, could be said to perpetuate

either a twin or a "foetus/placenta" kind of relatedness, both isolated inside their amniotic sac from the world around them— a world that they would then presumably be experiencing as an also phantasied but hostile and uncomprehending "prenatal mother"?

31. When a psychotic patient sees his own self or *"double"* projected in another corner of the room, could he be said to be hallucinating his own erstwhile and placental "double", with the room here again representing the womb? (On this notion or phenomenon of the "double" or the *"Doppelgänger"*, and of its possible prenatal connotations, see Aray & Bellagamba, 1971.) As I have not yet read it, I am not sure whether Rank's 1914 article entitled "Der Doppelgänger", contains any reference to the interest he was to later show in birth and prenatal life in general.

32. When the patient appears to treat and experience the analyst's office as the womb or the prenatal mother (Vesy-Wagner, 1966, p. 18), could the analyst himself represent in the transference the former placental companion or roommate, friend or foe, according to what the prenatal experience of it had been?

33. Could any reference to a *"boundary"*, a *"frontier"*, a *"demarcation line"*, and so on, be a symbolic allusion to the placental membrane, since the latter constitutes a commonly shared, anatomical and physiological boundary between mother and unborn child? A patient of mine once said that there was "always a thin barrier between people which must never be violated".

Whatever small advance we may be able to make, however, in our understanding of the ways in which some aspects of our postnatal life are often prefigured in, and sometimes shaped by, the way we react or are made to react in prenatal life, we shall need the work of analysts such as Fonagy (2001, 2003) before we can achieve a better understanding of what part our genotype plays not only in determining our response to the environment, but also in influencing the latter's response to us. In 1912, when Freud contrasted the way in which psychoanalysis had broadened our understanding of the influence on our psyche of what he called "accidental"—that is, environmental—"factors", he contrasted this with what it had been able to tell us concerning the role played by inherited factors, about which it knew "no more so far than is already known" (1912b, p. 99 n.). And yet, supposing that further psychoanalytic research did one day give us at least some reason for thinking that events as early as conception can be referred to in the material of patients as well as in myths, legends, art, and so on, and here again by means of the appropriate symbols, it would presumably be a very uncurious mind that did not then ask itself whether the events that take place at molecular level in each of the germ cells during their respective maturation into sperm and ovum—and which thus play such an important part in determining the composition of our genetic complement prior to conception—could not themselves sometimes be unconsciously communicated about, or find some kind of expression in, what our patients tell us, or the way they relate to us in sessions? Freud did in fact wonder (1916–17, p. 199) whether we might one day "succeed in distinguishing which portion of the latent mental processes is derived from the individual prehistoric period" (by which he presumably meant the earliest stages or ontogenic life) "and which from the phylogenic one". He went on to say: "It is not, I believe, impossible that we shall". Others have not been so optimistic.

A SHORT NOTE ON THE POSSIBLE SYMBOLISM OF HEREDITY

Several years ago I made a few attempts to see whether some of my patients had unwittingly been telling me something about their heredity and their way of handling it. I am not talking here about conscious communications, although when one of these patients once said to me that he felt he had been "dealt the wrong cards" but had perhaps not been able to make "the best use of those [he] had got", it was difficult not to ask myself whether he had been almost consciously referring to the so-called random distribution of genetic material (I say "so-called random" by way of paying due respect to those who feel there is a divine purpose in this distribution and that the Divinity surely does not simply play dice with the creation). I cannot recall whether I suggested this to my patient, nor, if so, what his response had been.

I also have in my notes two or three dreams that, although they had seemed to make perfectly good sense when interpreted at postnatal level and within the transference, seemed to me in retrospect to have also evoked in rather striking fashion some of the molecular events I referred to earlier. As I also realized later, the dream of this patient may have derived part of its relevance from the fact that the question of whether he was entitled to compensation hinged on whether psychiatrists came to the conclusion that his depression could be considered reactive (and hence deserving of compensation), or "endogenous"—that is, inherited, and hence unrelated to the damage incurred.

Is it too flippant to ask whether anyone, going back to playing cards once again, has ever raised the question of whether a psychoanalytic explanation could be found for the fascination exerted on keen card players by the game of bridge? Two people, who refer to each other as their "partner", sit opposite each other at a square table; and two other people, who also refer to each other as "my partner", sit opposite each other at the other sides of the table. Cards are dealt. The game then consists in an attempt, by the player whose "bid" has topped that of the other players, to play his or her cards and those of his or her partner (which now lie face upwards on the table) in such a way as to make the greater number of "tricks"—the role of the other couple being, of course, to try to prevent this. If we once again accept the possibility that the unconscious might use the dealing of cards to symbolize the random (?) distribution of genetic material, could we say that what we have here is a situation in which a couple of "partners" (parents?) do their best to match their "genes" (cards) against those of another couple and to do better than the latter by producing a greater number of "children" (tricks)? And, in the final analysis, does the exciting nature of the play owe something to the fact that the other couple may unconsciously represent one's own parents? Furthermore, when one member of the losing couple occasionally blames his or her partner for having played badly, does this repeat the unfortunately not unknown tendency of parents to blame each other for whatever disappointment their progeny may have caused them, or again for whatever may have caused them to remain a childless couple ("no tricks" in the case of a so-called "grand slam" by the other card playing couple)? And so on.

The frustration one feels when asking oneself questions of this sort comes from the fact that even when they do occasionally appear to admit of a possible answer and to thus increase the relevance of psychoanalysis to an understanding of "the mind", it is by no means easy, as I said earlier, to find a way in which such understanding can be used to give practical help to patients suffering from psychological difficulties or psychiatric disorders of one kind or another. As I have tried to show here, this is already true, to some extent, of any advance we may be able to make in our understanding of the prenatal conditioning of postnatal mental life and behaviour; but this will presumably be even more true of any advance we may be able to make in our understanding of the influence of our genotype on the unconscious. We may at first have to be guided by the ongoing research carried out by geneticists on the role played by hereditary factors in human mental life and behaviour, but this need not stop psychoanalysts and psychotherapists from doing a little research of their own, as Fonagy has shown. This will require an even greater tolerance of the uncertainly we already have to face in the case of prenatal research, but, as Freud said at the end of the introduction to his *New Introductory Lectures on Psychoanalysis* (1933a), anyone who works in the field of psychology must learn to endure the hardships of uncertainty even more than in any other field of inquiry.

NOTE

1. For earlier references to the placenta becoming "bad" and "poisonous", see DeMause, 1982, pp. 258–271, some of the material presented by my Patient A (chapter two), and also a renewed reference to DeMause in chapter five.

CHAPTER FIVE

Additional remarks about the literature concerned with prenatal life

The first work I wish to return to in this final chapter is Paul's 1983 paper, for it contained so much of what had been my own experience of certain patients that quoting further from it will make it possible to enlarge a little on what this experience had been.

1. Paul had speculated, for example, about whether the "frequent expectations of perfection rigidly maintained in schizoid patients" could have their origin in a persistent and insufficiently worked through longing to still be able to "maintain a functioning placenta" inside the maternal object (1983, p. 563). I had not known of Paul's paper when writing a 1984 paper on "some aspects of Kleinian theory", but I realize that the words just quoted had already expressed something not unlike my own speculations about the possible placental origins of the use of idealization in attempts to maintain the perfection of an object.

2. The blood-sucking, vampire-like, parasitical nature of foetal types of craving, which I thought had been so clearly in evidence in my Patient A (chapter two), is something that Paul

himself considers to be an important characteristic and marker of the foetal drive (1983, p. 564).

3. I also agree with Paul that the "adhesiveness" of certain transferences (1983, p. 561) could repeat the way in which the unborn child "adheres" to the uterine wall by means of its placenta. There is also a clear indication, in the passage just referred to, that Paul himself sees the conscious or unconscious fear that certain patients have of losing their contact with the analyst as sometimes repeating a fear of reliving in the transference what may have been the experience of having actually become detached from the uterine wall at birth, or of having nearly become detached from it as a result of a threatened miscarriage. Moreover, I think I may be right in saying that Paul, too, regards an "adhesive" type of transference as being itself one of the markers by which it might be possible to tell a prenatal type of relatedness from a mainly oral one (concerning "adhesiveness", see below my reference to Mitrani; and as regards the possible effect on a child of having nearly become detached from the uterine wall during a threatened miscarriage, see also Maiello, 2001).

4. There are several examples in Paul's paper of the various images, metaphors, terms of phrase, and so on that could be said to constitute what I sometimes think of as the "language" of prenatality, the decoding of which should, in principle, enable us to detect when a patient is telling us something about his or her prenatal life.

5. By his own use of the term "placental object", Paul (1983, p. 561) himself seems to me to have alluded, even if by implication only, to the possible existence of levels of transference in which patients could be regarded as sometimes seeking in the analyst, not only a prenatal mother kind of "object", but also that part of their prenatal self that had once enabled them to relate to this prenatal mother, namely their erstwhile and now lost placenta (see again, in this connection, Sidney Klein, 1980, p. 400; 1984, p. 313).

6. On page 556, Paul also mentioned how a patient of his had "likened his relationship to the analyst to the experience of a renal dialysis without which he could not live" (see below a reference

to another patient, whom Rosser described as "mourning" the loss of her dialysis machine after being given a kidney transplant.) Paul's implication was that an unconscious connection had taken place in the patient's mind between the analyst and the prenatal mother who had helped him get rid of his foetal wastes in prenatal life.

7. Paul, too (1983, pp. 556–557), like Bion (1980, pp. 104, 108), sees projective identification as operating already *in utero*, and I must here again express my regret not to have come across these two publications in time to be able to quote them in the already mentioned 1984 paper, which said more or less the same thing.

8. One of the most striking passages in Paul's 1983 paper concerns the kind of countertransference that patients who use prenatal mechanisms can sometimes elicit in the analyst. As I briefly mentioned in chapter one, he described, for example (pp. 558–559), how a patient of his had produced in him "reactions of hatred" that threatened to "lead to action", such as a "desire to strike out, to shout her down, to get rid of her in any way possible", and how further inquiry into the anamnesis had revealed that when giving birth to her, the patient's mother had developed secondary uterine inertia (p. 560). If I understand Paul correctly, his conclusion had been that he had come to feel increasingly "inert" himself—that is, no longer able to impart any kind of movement to a patient who had got "stuck" inside him—and that he had developed the kind of helplessness that would sometimes make us welcome the intervention of anyone who could get the patient "out of" us. The patient's mother, it was later revealed, had actually needed to be delivered of her by Caesarean section. (An almost identical example was once reported to me by Neville Symington from his own practice—1988, personal communication.)

What Paul has had to say in a later 1989 paper concerning what he believes to be the pre- and perinatal origins of a particularly severe superego and of the "penitential" "form of transference to which the latter sometimes gives rise" (pp. 43, 48, 68) seems to me not unlike what my Patient A had mentioned as her feeling of being in "some kind of prison"—a "prison" that, in spite of her having described it as self-imposed and as having had no other jailer than herself, had also appeared to represent the therapy as well as an unconsciously remembered persecutory and imprisoning kind of womb (see below, in connection to this, some thoughts about the possible perinatal origins of the "surrounding", "suffocating" and "crushing" form of superego described by Mason, 1983). Paul too, in his own 1989 paper, has used the word "crushing" to describe the mental pressure exerted by the kind of persecuting superego he sees as being responsible for what he has described as the "penitential" kind of transference; and in a 1990 paper on the "Phenomenology of Mental Pressure", he not only described how a patient had felt "surrounded" by this "pressure", but he also expressed fairly clearly his belief, if I have read him correctly, that such feelings of being "surrounded" and "crushed" could have been the reliving of a persecutory experience of birth (pp. 12–14).[1] This of course made me think of what my Patient A, in Session 16 of her second admission to hospital, had described as the sensation of being "surrounded", "suffocated", and "squeezed out" of the hospital by an ever-narrowing "circle" of nurses, and how this, too, had seemed to me to be the reliving of a persecutory birth experience.

Turning now to the question of whether the foetus could "be said to feel fear or aggression" (Bion, 1980, p. 78), I have already mentioned a few of the writers who could be said to have either explicitly or implicitly hinted at, or at least speculated about, the possible usefulness of conceiving of a prenatal form of aggressivity (for example, Blomfield, 1985, 1987; Grunberger, 1983; Sidney Klein, 1980, 1984; Paul, 1983; A. Rascovsky, 1956; A. Rascovsky et al., 1971b). Although there is a certain variation in what these writers have implied to be the "object" of such aggressivity—some mentioning the placenta, others the prenatal mother herself as the main object of foetal libido and aggressivity—their very use of the term "object" almost amounts to a statement about the possible existence of object-directed prenatal forms of relatedness that would precede, albeit at physiological level to start with, the type of object relationships that are at present generally conceived as coming into being for the first time when the baby makes its first entry, at birth, into the world of postnatal life. I am not sure, however, whether one can make the same assumption in the case of Grunberger, one of the writers to whom I have referred. I quoted him as having written about a "foetal aggressivity" ["*l'aggressivité du foetus*"] (1983, p. 926), which has as its object the body of the mother and, in particular, the inside of that body ["*qui a le corps de la mère pour objet et, en particulier, l'intérieur de celui-ci*"]. A more careful reading of this paper, however, makes one see that the reproduction of this primitive aggressivity in the "analytic situation", as well as the foetal narcissism that goes together with it, is not regarded by Grunberger as being grounded on any "objectal" form of relatedness ["*elle n'est étayée par aucune relation objectale*"] (p. 925). I have not yet been able to read Grunberger's 1989 book entitled *New Essays on Narcissism*, but its 1990 review by Frosh would appear to indicate that Grunberger does indeed regard the foetal state—contrary to what I had at first assumed—as some kind of "prenatal Eden" (Frosh p. 193) in which aggressivity, therefore, would presumably be deemed not to play too great a part, if any. I have felt it necessary to go into this in some detail because I would not like, by focusing exclusively on Grunberger's mention of a "foetal aggressivity" that has as its "object" the inside of the mother's body, to attribute to him a meaning he may not have intended.

I do not know whether Segal would explicitly subscribe to the idea of a primary type of aggressivity by which the unborn child could be conceived as physiologically "attacking" the mother's body *from within*; however, what sometimes appears to be a patient's tendency to re-enact a prenatal mode of relatedness and behaviour seems to me almost hinted at in the material she presented from a patient (1983). In one of his dreams the latter had described a room with a "funny", "round", concave kind of ceiling that he had associated "to a womb" (p. 273). In another dream (p. 274) he was beside a "beautiful pool". A dog had "shat in the pool", and the patient's father had "removed the shit". Segal had interpreted the "beautiful pool" as representing what the patient had already shown signs of experiencing as the good aspects of the analysis and of Segal herself. The dog, she had suggested, had stood for the patient's destructive side, one that wanted to soil, out of envy, an analysis he perceived as "beautiful and rich" (p. 274). The father who had "removed the shit" had been interpreted as the admired but also envied analyst whose "father" aspect was not allowing the patient's envious and destructive part—represented here again by the dog—to "get away with" this soiling.

Segal did not explicitly refer to what seems to me to have been the possible amniotic and hence prenatal connotations of the pool, but bearing in mind the fact that although most of the foetus' waste products are eliminated into the mother's body via the placenta, a certain amount of these—mostly urine—goes directly into the amniotic "pool". Would this allow one to say that Segal had described the way in which her patient, after regressing in his dream to the stage when his erstwhile foetal self had in reality emptied its wastes into the mother's body, had then used the dream to describe not only his feeling of being inside Segal's body, but also his wish to soil it from within, precisely because of his envy of its being so "beautiful and rich"?

The work of DeMause has also been mentioned already, but I should like to make two additional points. At the end of his book *Foundations of Psychohistory* (1982, pp. 258—260), DeMause developed his concept of what he called the "nurturant [i.e. good and nourishing] placenta" as opposed to the "poisonous [i.e. bad and persecutory] placenta".[2] This reminded me of what usually seemed to be my Patient A's efforts to maintain an image of me as a good intra-uterine and placental kind of companion and ally in the "womb" of my office, but also of the other moments when she seemed to be experiencing me as a placenta that had been "poisoned" by the information I obtained about her from the nurses, and hence as a "me" she felt might sometimes be in collusion with the latter to "squeeze" her out of the hospital as in some kind of miscarriage or premature labour.

I was also interested in DeMause's speculation (1982, p. 260) about whether the "poisonous placenta", by reason of its being the first "punitive agency", could be regarded as a forerunner of what Melanie Klein described as the "bad breast", the persecutory aspects of which, she suggested, could be conceived as constituting the nucleus and starting point from which all superego structures and functions later develop (1932, pp. 194–198, 213, 1945, pp. 379, 388, 1952a, p. 210): a nucleus and starting point that she had regarded as beginning to form around the middle of the first year after birth (1957, pp. 179, 219).

Still concerning the superego, I made a brief allusion earlier to a 1983 paper by Mason[3] and what seems to me to be this writer's useful proposal concerning the possibility of conceiving of a "surrounding", "suffocating", "crushing" type of superego (p. 143). We normally visualize the superego as arising from the internalization of the various parental, educational, religious, and social dos and don'ts to which we are exposed from early childhood onwards; and Melanie Klein has shown how its formation can also be contributed to by the various often part-object "introjects" that get into our psyche almost from birth, or at least towards "the middle of the first year". If I am right in this, it would seem that we therefore tend to visualize the superego as a structure that is "inside" the psyche rather than one that "surrounds" it. Basing himself on clinical material, however, Mason has identified aspects of the superego that he convincingly demonstrates can create in the subject a feeling of being actually "surrounded" and "closed in" upon by this superego "from all sides", and the "crushing" and "suffocating" effect of this that engenders in the subject a feeling of "hopelessness" from which "no escape is possible" except by "panic and explosion". Mason then adds, with the help here again of clinical material, how this surrounding, closing in, and suffocating superego could play a part in conditions such as asthma, claustrophobic anxieties, psychotic breakdowns, and the feeling of suffocating within a constricting sort of "skin" (pp. 163–165). The word "skin" invites, of course, a comparison with the work of Anzieu: could one conceive of a "skin superego", a "surmoi-Peau"? I return to this in a moment.

As in the case of DeMause (1982), Mason's proposals have made me think of my Patient A, whose material appears to have confirmed their usefulness. The severity of her superego had already been suggested by a remark she had made as early as Session 6 of her first hospital admission: "I have destroyed my parents and should be destroyed myself." In view of her insistence, at some later point of the therapy, that her "prison" was entirely self-imposed, I had eventually speculated about the possibility of some feeling of guilt that she had to expiate and which, I later realized, could have had something to do with whatever "horrific things" of her past she had been unable or unwilling to talk about—to say nothing about the possible feeling of guilt resulting from her concealment of those "things". In Session 16 of her second hospital admission, she had described a feeling of being "closed in" upon by a hostile and ever-narrowing "circle" of nurses that was trying to "suffocate" and even "kill" her. She had not used the word "crushing", but as this constricting "circle" had been described as "bearing down" on her and as trying to "squeeze" her out of the hospital, I had seen this as the possible reliving of a persecutory, and hence possibly "crushing", birth kind of experience. Furthermore, her "psoriasis" had made her feel attacked "from all sides" by her skin, and the pain, which she had described as "enveloping", had therefore "surrounded" her. The "death" that, she felt, was still trying to "get" her when she was inside her "cocoon" (Session 16) had also made me think of Victor Hugo's poem about the persecuting "eye" of "conscience"—that is, the superego—which had followed Cain right into the sealed tomb in which he had hoped to find a refuge from it. I was naturally interested to see that Mason had made a similar point about the persecutory "eye" or "eyes" of the "surrounding superego" (p. 143). Finally, Mason has also written (1983, p. 164) about the way in which patients who cut themselves may be trying to let a bit of themselves, in the form of blood, escape from a feeling of being imprisoned within a persecutory "skin superego": a possibility I had considered myself when examining the possible reasons for my Patient A's attempts to obtain relief by cutting herself. Mason's own work, like that of Paul, would therefore appear to have moved in directions similar to my own.

Returning to the interest that DeMause, too, has expressed in the possible prenatal or perinatal origins of a "punitive" and unhelpful kind of superego, what he had in mind was not so much the possible effect of a persecutory and surrounding birth-giving mother, as that of a placenta that had ceased to be "nurturant" and become "poisonous" (1982, p. 260). My drawing a parallel (in chapter three) between placental functions and those of the postnatal ego does not have to clash with DeMause's view about the "poisonous" placenta being a possible forerunner of the superego. One could imagine a postnatal "ego" as continuing to exercise the placenta's more helpful aspects, and a punitive superego its potentially unhelpful ones.

As I mentioned in chapter one, what Grotstein had written about the "diabolical parasitism" of certain patients (1978, p. 141) and their requiring "interpretations that acknowledge their experience of unbornness and their difficulty and/or reluctance in finding their way to a metaphoric 'birth canal'" (p. 144) had all seemed to me to be an almost explicit allusion to the possible existence and interpretability of prenatal levels of transference. What also interested me in Grotstein's paper is a discussion of another paper of that same year by Langs (1978) concerning the "bipersonal field"—the term introduced by W. and M. Baranger to refer to the exchanges that take place between patient and analyst in the analytic situation, as well as to the "space" within which these exchanges take place. As it is to that "space" to which Grotstein seems to have been referring when writing about the "space" for "symbolic transference illusion" (1978, p. 146), his description of it is perhaps relevant here. He first compared this "space" for illusion (p. 141) to an "interactional interface between the two members of the dyad" (p. 142) and then referred to it as a "highly dynamic membrane where the symbolic exchanges occur" (p. 142).[4] In an earlier work, Langs had also written about the "interface of interaction between the patient and the analyst" and described this interface as an "ever-changing hypothetical surface or line which is determined by and, in turn, determines the nature and implications of the respective communication between patient and analyst and receives continuous input, in varying proportions, from each" (1976, vol. 2, pp. 578–579).

What strikes me here is that both these descriptions, those by Langs and Grotstein, respectively, could serve as a description of the placental membrane that separates the blood of the foetus from that of the mother inside the placenta. The placental membrane, too, can be regarded as a "highly dynamic"—although this time by no means "hypothetical"—"interface" or "line" that separates the two members of the foetus/mother "dyad", "receives continuous input, in varying proportions, from each", and is now believed, as mentioned earlier, to play an active role in "determining the nature of these exchanges as well as the rate at which they occur" (Page, 1963, p. 147). Could it therefore be argued that, in the passages I have just quoted, both Langs and Grotstein may have unwittingly but intuitively sensed and described what could be regarded as the postnatal continuation, in psychological form, of both the existence and function of this "highly dynamic" placental "surface", "line", and "interface"?

Correspondingly, and by the same token, could one also conceive the "space" inside the placenta—the so-called "intervillous spaces"—as being likewise re-created, in psychological form, by the "space for symbolic transference illusion" to which Grotstein had referred in his own paper: the only difference being that here again there is, of course, nothing "illusory" about the physiological (or proto-psychological?) exchanges that take place in these placental intervillous spaces between the blood of the foetus and that of the mother.[5]

Mahler herself could perhaps be said to have unwittingly alluded to the placental membrane—this common boundary between mother and unborn child—when she defined "symbiosis" (1967, p. 742) as a state of "omnipotent fusion with the representation of the mother" involving "a delusion of *common boundary* of the two actually and physically separate individuals" (emphasis added). Ammon (1974, p. 54), too, has described the boundary between "the ego and the outside world"—that is, between the "me" and the "not me"—as an "active biological membrane the function of which is not only to separate the outside world from the internal one" (I presume that by the latter Ammon had meant the "self"), but to also "allow for some communication between the two" (translated for this edition). The notion of "adhesive identification" proposed by Bick (1968) and later taken up by Meltzer (1975) could perhaps be regarded, as Paul himself has suggested (1983), as an unwitting reference to that aspect of prenatal life whereby the maternal face of the placenta "adheres" to the uterine wall—an adhesion that, if incomplete or disrupted, would cause haemorrhage and put the foetus' life at risk. (See also below for a reference to Mitrani's 1994, 1995a, proposals about the conceivability of "adhesive pseudo-object" types of relationships.)

Freud's concept of the "protective shield" (1920g, p. 29ff) was extended by Khan to denote the kind of shield that the early postnatal mother interposes between the infant and the outside world (1974, pp. 44–51). Could this concept be extended even further to include a reference to prenatal "shielding"—one that could be seen as comprising two, if not three, kinds of shield: the mother's body, the womb inside that body, and, last but not least, the placental membrane or "barrier" that normally "protects" the foetus from possible immunological clashes with the maternal blood inside the placenta?

I have mentioned before how modern theories about "mirroring" (Kohut, 1971; Pines, 1984) could perhaps be extended to include a notion according to which not only the foetus' blood, but also its sense of "self", could be conceived as being projected onto and into the placenta via the two umbilical arteries and then sent back to the foetal body via the umbilical vein—thus leading to a notion of a placental and biological kind of "mirroring" and of a "reflected" sense of self that could be experienced as either "good" or "bad", pleasant or unpleasant, depending on whether or not the pregnancy was progressing favourably; and how it might not be too far-fetched to look upon this kind of physical "reflection" as preparing the ground for a later and more perfected ability to "reflect" in the "thinking" and "reflection" sense of the word.

I also mentioned in "Review of previous work" in chapter one what seemed to be Joseph's own recognition (1983) of the role possibly played by unresolved foetal longings in those forms of psychic "pain" that could be traced to the separation from the mother at birth (p. 100). Her 1982 paper on "Addiction to Near Death" has, moreover, put me in mind of how my Patient A's apparent compulsion to destroy herself, her frequent perception of the womb as a place of death, and in particular her attempt to commit suicide in a locked public lavatory (Session 3 of her second hospital admission). It had made me wonder whether she could have had an actual "near-death" experience *in utero*, which she had then been compelled to repeat; and if so, whether experiences of "near death" *in utero* could leave a trace in the unconscious and partly explain what happened in the cases observed by Joseph? The dream (Joseph, 1982, pp. 450–451), in which the patient could not "allow himself" to get out of a "long" and "dark" cave, "almost a cavern", could then perhaps be significant in that respect? What Joseph also described in that paper as the perverse kind of excitement involved in such self-destructive forms of acting out has itself reminded me of the "sense of excitement" my Patient A once told me she derived from hiding in her cocoon and not letting people know what she was thinking.

Returning once again to Grotstein, it seems to me that his aforementioned proposal of a "dual-track" or "Siamese-twin" analogy as a way of conceiving mental development and functioning could here again be likened to what I recalled earlier as his obvious awareness of the possibility of sometimes turning to intra-uterine life when searching for a better understanding of postnatal mental life and behaviour. As I cannot hope to be able to do justice to the full import of Grotstein's contribution to our understanding of the mind in terms of projective and introjective mechanisms and the way in which they can operate along the lines of what he calls the "dual-track" "principle" or "model", I shall only use one passage of his writings in order to illustrate what I mean by saying that the "dual-track" type of functioning could perhaps reflect what had once been a prenatal reality.

The passage in question, at the end of Grotstein's book, *Splitting and Projective Identification*, reads:

> Projective identification is best understood by the application of the dual-track principle involving the symbiotic "Siamese Twin" model in which there can be two states of mind simultaneously on two different levels: one of separateness and one of fusion. Thus the infant can go back and forth between the two states of experience or experience both states simultaneously. [1981, p. 214]

My reason for thinking that this "dual-track" kind of functioning could be conceived as having already started in the womb is as further described below.

What Grotstein seems to me to have in mind when he speaks of a state of "separateness" and one of "fusion" is the condition of being "separated from", or "fused with", what he has referred to elsewhere as the "background object of primary identification" (1978, p. 146), which he sees as "most closely associated with the womb-mother" (1983b, p. 496). If we therefore assume the existence of a prenatal "sense of self", which, I think, Grotstein might be prepared to do in view of what he has to say about foetal consciousness (1983a p. 403), this prenatal sense of self could presumably be conceived as comprising, not only a "foetal" sense of self that would be located in the foetal body proper, but also a "placental" sense of self that would be located in the placenta, the two being linked together, "Siamese-twin" fashion, by the umbilical cord. Whereas the foetal body proper could be regarded as having already achieved, even at that early stage, a state of relative "separateness" from the "womb-mother", the placental "self", by contrast, would of course have to be seen as still being in a state of "fusion", literally, with the uterine wall. By the same token, the foetus as a whole—that is, foetal body *and* placenta—could presumably be seen as capable of not only experiencing its "sense of self" as going "back and forth", along what could be called the "dual-track" of the umbilical cord, between a relative state of "separateness" from and a state of "fusion with" this prenatal "womb-mother", but of also being able, presumably, to experience "both states simultaneously". I am aware, however, that what Grotstein may have had in mind when proposing his "dual-track" or "Siamese-twin" theory of mental development may be different from the representation I have formed of it through his writings. If that is the case, what I have just said about it being perhaps an intuitive description of the continuation, in postnatal mental life, of something that has started in the womb, will have to be amended or may not even apply.

Like others before her, Brownscombe Heller (1989, p. 157) has rightly used the word "metabolizing" to refer to the psychological function whereby, as Bion suggested, a good and loving mother contains within herself the sometimes disturbing feelings aroused in her by her infant's rages or distress and hopefully responds to these in a calm, caring, thinking kind of way that then not only causes the infant to unconsciously incorporate and identify with this calm and loving mother and to thus develop a capacity for self-containment himself, but also provides him with the external and internal environment in which his initially primitive, raw, chaotic perception can gradually become capable of the kind of change that makes ego growth possible. The word "metabolizing" could, however, also be used, and without recourse to metaphor, to describe the physical processes by which the also "containing" body of the pregnant mother receives the wastes of her unborn child and provides the latter with the oxygen and nutrients it needs to survive and grow—processes that some writers have suggested could be regarded as the origins of the mechanisms identified by Melanie Klein and others as "projection", "identification", "projective identification", "introjection", and so on. (For the possible prenatal origins of these various mechanisms see, for example, Bion, 1980, pp. 104, 108; Blomfield, 1985, pp. 303–304; Paul, 1983, pp. 556–557; Ployé, 1984; Whyte, 1991.)

Still concerning the placenta's function as an eliminator of foetal wastes, Rosser made the interesting observation that when patients on renal dialysis eventually receive a kidney transplant, they may, following this, become depressed and literally mourn the machine that has kept them alive until then. Rosser (Kind, Rosser, & Williams, 1982, p. 166) described how one of these patients had come to depend on the machine "as a child on its mother", felt it to "share and understand her feelings", and had, moreover, continued to visit it daily after being "severed from it by the transplant". Rosser made no specific mention of the prenatal mother, but since one of the latter's functions is precisely to "dialyse" and "detoxify" the blood of her unborn child, one cannot help wondering whether what this patient had been mourning as a result of being "severed" from the machine had been the mother who had kept her blood free from urea before birth and to whom she had once again, in the form of the machine, become "attached", emotionally as well as physically. The "detoxifying" function of the analyst has itself been frequently referred to in analytic writings (Bryce Boyer, 1978, p. 68), and this, together with the above considerations, seems to be yet another reason for exploring the possible existence of levels of transference in which patients might be trying to use the analyst or therapist as a prenatal mother kind of "machine" or even, as I and others have suggested (see Sidney Klein, 1980, p. 400, 1984, p. 313), as a replacement for that part of their prenatal self in which part of these dialysing and detoxifying processes had first begun to take place: namely, their erstwhile and long-lost placenta (the major part of the detoxifying process takes place, of course, in the mother herself—that is, her kidneys).

Bowlby, too (1958), could, I think, be included among the writers who have told us something, albeit sometimes unwittingly, concerning prenatal life. Like Balint (1951, pp. 144–145) and many others, Bowlby had pointed out that there was more to the "child's tie to his mother" that the orally centred forms of attachment so thoroughly studied by Melanie Klein and her followers. What he had been particularly interested in was the part that could be played in this "tie" by the phylogenetically transmitted instincts of what he called "attachment", this last word being at the very centre of his theoretical and clinical work. Considering that one of the most striking features of the child's "tie" to its mother before birth is that it is physically "attached" to her by the umbilical cord, and despite Bowlby's scepticism about what he once referred to as the "hypothetical craving to return to the mother's womb" (1958, p. 369), I cannot help wondering whether his emphasis on "attachment" could not be extended to include some reference to the umbilical "tie" or "attachment". The hypothesis of an intermediary, umbilical stage of "attachment" would seem to me to constitute an acceptable theoretical bridge between the "instincts" studied by Bowlby, and the postnatal, orally centred forms of attachment described by Melanie Klein. The setting up of such a bridge would not appear to impair in any way the value of these two writers' findings and might, in fact, establish some continuity between the two.

Winnicott himself could be mentioned here in connection with what was touched upon earlier concerning modern theories about "mirroring". I believe that Winnicott (1967) may well have been the first to do full justice to the "mirroring" role played in early postnatal life by the mother's face, and to the importance that the latter's expressiveness—or lack or it—can play in stimulating—or stunting—the baby's emotional and mental growth, its capacity to love, feel loved, feel recognized, and so on. Of course, other factors—such as the mother's voice and general handling of the baby—play a part in this as well, but as far as the mother's face is concerned, could one suppose that its role has a precursor in the one that the placenta had already played in "reflecting" to the unborn child a hopefully improved "image" of itself by providing "good" oxygen and nutrients in exchange for "bad" foetal wastes—in the same way as, after birth, "good" smiles and a kind voice will hopefully respond to "bad" screams and rages?

Mention was also made earlier of Neville Symington's remark (1983, p. 287) that analyst and patient could be regarded as forming a "single system" or a "corporate personality", with the analyst becoming, so to speak, "lassoed" to the patient's "illusory world" and hence running the risk of becoming a "victim" of this kind of relatedness more than would be the case in a "average social contact". I had added that this seemed to me to be particularly true of prenatal forms of relatedness, in which the umbilical cord could be said to play the role of this "lasso". No reference can be made to Symington's work, however, without also mentioning his contribution to the problem of narcissism (1993). He remarks that "people who have been through a terrible trauma . . . deal with it by inserting themselves into the [traumatizing] agent", and that they can thus be said to "live in a cocoon", or a kind of "narcissistic envelope" (p. 77).

This, too, has made me think of my Patient A. She had ensconced herself into what she had hoped would be the safe "envelope" or "cocoon" of a phantasied prenatal mother and a mother who may, in her case, well have been the "traumatizing agent"; but in spite of having found that even there "death" was trying to "get" her. She had then had the greatest difficulty in getting out of this cocoon, which, as she said, had become a kind of "prison". In spite of her insistence on the fact that this prison was entirely of her own making and that it had nothing to do with me, there was much to suggest that she also felt imprisoned inside a phantasied and persecutory "prenatal mother"/me from very early on—that is, from the time that the initial feeling of being inside me as in a safe cocoon had begun to wear off. The problem had then become one of helping her to get out. This seems to me remarkably similar to what Symington has also described as the "kind of war" that then develops between analyst and patient, with the analyst "trying to haul the patient" out of the cocoon and the patient "pulling for all his worth in the other direction" in an effort to stay where he is (p. 77). My patient was to succeed eventually in "hauling herself out" of the "prenatal mother"/me with her own "resources", although this seems to have been helped by her realizing that I was not going to give in to her plea for me to become her "friend" as a way of solving the problem.

The point I am trying to make here is that it is difficult in such cases not to think of the problems often created by a difficult birth. As I said earlier, the pressure that Miss A must have felt me to be putting on her by resisting her pleas for "friendship" may at the perinatal level have been unconsciously experienced by her as the beginning of a uterine contraction that had then had the effect of giving her the anger-driven energy she needed in order to get herself out of the hitherto imprisoning "prenatal mother"/me.

A key concept in Symington's theory of narcissism is that of the "life giver" (1993, pp. 35, 37, 81–82). If I understand him correctly, opting for the "life giver" is to opt for a non-narcissistic kind of "position", and hence for one that is presumably similar to what we mean by a true object relationship. Before I mention how this has once again led me back to my experience of my Patient A, perhaps I can make use of what Grotstein had said, in his "Foreword" to Symington's book on narcissism, about the difference that he himself (Grotstein) thought could be made between a "true" object relationship and a "narcissistic" one. To quote Grotstein's own words: ". . . the narcissist uses the object, not in a normal sharing relationship for normal dependency and interdependency, but for a manipulative, parasitic relationship in which the object is to be seduced and controlled so as to allow the autistic/narcissistic subject to remain omnipotent and protectively encapsulated" (Symington, 1993, p. xvi).

Although in the closing phase of her "therapy" Miss A's pleas for me to relax my analytic stance had seemed to be a desperate attempt to re-create with me the "close" relationship she had had with her father as a child (and at the same time escape from what she seemed to experience as the "prison" of a persecutory "prenatal mother"/me), these pleas had also seemed to have constituted a striking example of what she had previously described, in one of the early sessions of her second hospital admission, as her tendency to "manipulate people". Some earlier "manipulation" of me could also be said to have been carried out by her use of the "cocoon" (which prevented others from knowing what she was thinking), as well as by what she was to describe, in Session 39 of her second admission, as her ability to distance herself from people by "giving out psychotic stuff"—as well, perhaps, as the prenatal "stuff" she could see I was interested in. Could one therefore suppose that by "giving out" material that had made me repeatedly talk to her about a still active, prenatal and "parasitic" side of her personality, she had unconsciously striven to maintain some "omnipotent" kind of "control" over me but at the same time, by doing this, had created the very kind of interpretive and prenatal "prison" from which she was consciously trying to escape? (She had herself remarked, in the second admission, that her "manipulating people" put her "in the position of being controlled by others"). By the same token, her resistance to my suggestion that the prison was also experienced as myself could likewise be regarded as a struggle not to fall a prey to what she unconsciously experienced as my attempt to "control" her by means of interpretations that presented me as persecutory, and which she resented because of her fear of experiencing me as "bad" or dangerous.

I briefly referred earlier to the possible usefulness of conceiving of two types of prenatal transferences: those in which the "prenatal mother" could be deemed to be the main transference "object", and others in which the therapist appeared to be treated as the patient's erstwhile placenta. Could one say that in the former, prenatally regressed though he may be, the patient could be regarded as still able to make a comparatively non-narcissistic choice by relating to a truly "non-self", "life giving" mother? And in the second, postulated, "placental", more regressed type of prenatal transference, could the patient be regarded as making a narcissistic choice by making the therapist play the role of his—that is, the patient's own—discarded or disowned placental self? Another possible way of saying more or less the same thing could of course consist in pointing out that in the prenatal "position", the real "life giver" is, of course, the mother herself, and that the placenta is only an intermediary or vehicle between her and the unborn child.

One could also perhaps once again consider here the "mirroring" types of transference, as well as the personality of Narcissus himself, who had preferred the reflection of his face in the pond to the charms of the Nymph "Echo". I recalled earlier the possibility of comparing the placenta to a "mirror" that, stuck on the uterine "wall", "reflects" to the unborn child what one hopes to be "good" oxygen and nutrients in exchange for "bad" foetal wastes. If we were to combine this "mirror" analogy with the possibility of also conceiving of a particularly regressed form of prenatal transference in which the patient would be using the therapist as a "placental" extension of his own self more than as a truly "non-self" prenatal mother "object", one could loosely compare such a patient to someone who, in passing a shop window, is more interested in using this window as a mirror in which to check his or her appearance than in looking through it to see the various objects that lie beyond it. By the same token, a patient who was really interested in what the therapist had to say could be compared to someone who looked *through* the window, went into the shop to see at closer quarters what it contained, and perhaps made a purchase. An analogy of this sort, suitably adapted, could, I think, describe several of the various situations that come up in analysis or therapy, including, of course, those in which an envious patient goes into the analyst's metaphorical "shop" not to buy, but to wreck the place and make the therapist feel that he (the therapist) has nothing good to offer: a type of situation that—as Spillius remarked in her 1993 paper on "Varieties of Envious Experience"—every analyst must have encountered at one time or another in his or her career.

In his book *The Skin-Ego* (1989), Anzieu reports the case of a patient ("Zénobie"), who had wanted to know everything about him and whom he had described as having formed with him a "mirroring" kind of transference (*"un transfert en miroir"*, 1985, p. 220).[6] I could not at first understand how that patient could have used Anzieu as a "mirror" in which to see a reflection of herself while at the same time wanting to know everything about him—this sounded at first a little contradictory—but Anzieu explained that she had wanted to know everything about him only because she needed to ascertain whether her words were finding an echo in him; if they did, this then helped her to form an image of him that helped her, in turn, to form an image of her own self (1985, p. 200). Zénobie could thus perhaps be said to have provided an example of what Grotstein had mentioned, in his Foreword to Symington's book on Narcissism, as the way in which the narcissist controls the object for his own ends.

One more remark, perhaps, about what I suggested earlier might be the usefulness, when dealing with a "mirror" form of transference, of trying to see whether the patient could be showing signs of not only being prenatally regressed, but of also forming with the therapist the postulated sub-type of prenatal transference in which the patient would be using the therapist as a mainly "placental" object, and one that thus functions as a "mirror" in which the patient unconsciously hopes to find a pleasing and reassuring "reflection" of himself.

Both Anzieu and Pines have shown their own interest in the possible existence of a connection, however vague, between mirroring transferences and some unconscious wish, in the patients concerned, to re-create and recapture something of their intra-uterine life. Anzieu has not, admittedly, made a direct link between the two, but in his vivid and moving description of the behaviour of autistic children (1985, pp. 230–231), he wrote about what seems to be their attempt to artificially extend and prolong the feeling of still having an intra-uterine kind of "envelope" and to thus maintain the illusion of not having been born (p. 231). Since Anzieu's thoughts about the "enveloping" role of the "skin-ego" had obviously played an important part in his handling of the "mirroring" transference of his patient Zénobie (pp. 218–224), this seems to me to suggest that Anzieu himself probably saw the intra-uterine "envelope" as not only continuing itself in the "skin-ego", but as also providing some kind of disposition or *"Anlage"* for future and "mirroring" forms of transference (see also Anzieu, 1990).

Still in connection with "mirroring" and its possible prenatal origins, Pines had expressed his interest in whether the "bath of sound", or any other excitations in which one may be "immersed" from *"intra-uterine* and postnatal life onwards" (emphasis added) could be said to constitute an early and "biological" form of "mirroring",[7] which then continues in the more psychological forms of "mirroring" observed in certain transferences (1992, p. 25).

As far as I can see, Wright's 1991 book *Vision and Separation* has not made any reference to the possibility of some prenatal kind of "mirroring", but this author too has obviously given much thought to the mirroring that takes place between mother and child in early infancy, and to the role that the loving smile of a mother's face in particular can be said to play in helping the child develop the sense of a valued self (pp. 11–22). In contrast to this, mirroring can, of course, have its unpleasant side, and in describing the way in which the reflection of ourselves from somebody's face can become persecutory, Wright evoked Sartre's notion of the "Other", and how the presence of the "Other" can be experienced as a threat (pp. 30–31). In Wright's own words (p. 32), but referring to Sartre's ideas on the subject, "the Other on whom I depend for myself can also be my mortal enemy. He is feared because he threatens to annihilate my subjective self and re-organize the world in terms of his subjectivity, with me as an object". As Wright points out, Sartre described the experience of being "looked at" or "into" by this "Other" as taking place in postnatal life, which in present day terminology would then presumably mean that the subject was being the victim of some invasive and projective kind of identification on the part of this "Other". On the other hand, if we accept the possibility that the foetal "self", too, might sometimes be the victim of whatever adverse maternal factors may be impacting on its sense of security and "wholeness", one could suppose that what Sartre had described as the threatening power of "the Look" (Wright, 1991, p. 30) could be the revival and reproduction in postnatal life of a possible early experience of having felt threatened and invaded by a prenatal kind of "Other". Envisaging such a possibility would, of course, necessitate asking oneself whether the foetus can sometimes become "aware of certain 'things' that are 'not-self'" (Bion, 1980, p. 27); and it is hardly necessary to add that much clinical work will be needed before one could form any idea of whether interpreting certain transferences at those levels can be of some benefit to the patient.

I should now like to turn to the proposals that have been put forward by Ogden (1988, 1989b) and Mitrani (1994, 1996), respectively, about the possible usefulness of conceiving of early forms of relationship that would precede and be more primitive than what a large number of analysts and therapists, following Melanie Klein, have come to think of as the early "paranoid–schizoid" and "depressive" positions: the former referring to the infant's experience of, and way of relating to, its mother during the first or six months of postnatal life, and the latter referring to the depression that is then assumed to take place in the infant as a result of some gradual realization that the "good" and loved maternal breast and the "bad" and hated maternal breast are in fact one and the same breast, and that whether the infant likes it or not, it has to accept that something "good" can also be experienced as "bad".[8]

Ogden has, for example, suggested that it might be useful to postulate the existence of what he described as an "autistic–contiguous position", "more primitive than either the paranoid–schizoid or the depressive position" (1989b, p. 138), but which could also, for reasons that he developed (pp. 128–129), be regarded as an early "object" relationship. Ogden does not, however, see this "position" as corresponding to any particular stage of development. I find this a little puzzling because, as he himself indicated (pp. 129–130), there are certain similarities between the type of "object" involved in the postulated "autistic–contiguous position", and the "autistic" object as described by Tustin: the "auto-sensuous" phase described by the latter had, after all, been conceived by her as being most probably associated with sensations occurring during the prenatal stage (1991, p. 585).

Ogden explains (1989b, p. 128) that one of his reasons for making "contiguity" one of the main features or markers of the "autistic–contiguous position" is that in this particular psychological mode, the "principal medium through which connections are made and organizations achieved" is "the experience of surfaces touching one another".[9] At first, this made me think of what must be the important (and new) experience for the unborn child, when it becomes big enough to fill the whole of the uterine cavity, of feeling the "surface" of its skin coming into contact with, and therefore "touching", the "surface" of the womb's own inner "skin" or lining.[10] (Below I have more to say about another way of looking at Ogden's "autistic–contiguous position", aware though I am that he himself does not see it as corresponding to any particular developmental stage.[11])

Ogden has likewise presented some very moving clinical material (1989b p. 130) from his treatment of a blind schizophrenic adolescent who had insisted on holding his head against the hard edge of Ogden's chair to "provide some degree of boundedness" for himself. Ogden naturally related this search for hardness and "boundedness" to the way in which the boy had banged his head "against the hard edge of his crib" as a baby "in response to the disintegrating effect of long periods of disconnectedness from his mother"; but I also found myself thinking that my Patient A had herself sometimes felt an urge to "bash" her head against hard surfaces that appeared to be substitutes for me; and this, coupled with her feeling of being imprisoned inside a persecutory "prenatal mother"/me, had made me wonder whether she had wanted to re-create the sensation of having had her head pressed against the "hard", bony, "bounding" walls of her mother's imprisoning pelvis during labour and to thus demonstrate to me the pain as well as the rage of feeling trapped inside me.[12]

Turning now to Mitrani, I mentioned in chapter one her proposal (1994, 1996, pp. 151–203) about the possible usefulness of conceiving of an early form of relatedness that could, she suggested, be described as an "adhesive pseudo-object relationship", the main feature of which is the fact that, contrary to what obtains in our conception of a true object, "no space" appears to the observer to exist between subject and object. In Mitrani's own words: ". . . the superimposition of subject and object is so complete . . . that the concepts of 'otherness' or 'space' have little or no relevance" (1996, pp. 165–166). She then goes on to say (p. 167) that, whereas in "normal/narcissistic object relations" the object is still experienced as having a separate existence and the subject's awareness of this separateness is "tolerated to a greater or lesser extent", the mere "flicker" of such awareness in the "adhesive pseudo-object relationship" is not tolerated at all; "self and object remain largely undifferentiated—they are one and the same". Furthermore, disconnection from the object brings about a feeling of "catastrophic collapse" or a "dreadful sensation of being ripped out and thrown away" (p. 170).

It is this absence of "space" between subject and object that therefore accounts for Mitrani's use of the word "adhesive" to refer to this particular "pseudo" form of object relationship; and she describes (pp. 152–164) how this notion of "adhesiveness", together with the feeling of "total disintegration" that results from disconnection from the object, can be traced to the writings of Anzieu (1989, 1990), Bick (1968), Deutsch (1942), Gaddini (1969), Meltzer (1975, 1978, 1986), Ogden (1988, 1989a, 1989b), Tustin (1981, 1986, 1991), and Winnicott (1949, 1960).

Mitrani has also given us a clear description of what she sees as yet another difference between the reactions caused by the breakdown of "normal/narcissistic object relations" and those caused by the breakdown of "adhesive pseudo-object" types of relatedness. In the first, separation from the object causes the subject to react "with either neediness or a tight-fisted control of need through the use of tyranny and seduction" (1996, p. 169); but although the neediness and the loss of omnipotence creates a feeling of rejection (p. 170), it is not experienced as life-threatening. In the breakdown of an "adhesive", pseudo-object type of relatedness, on the other hand, the loss of omnipotence is experienced as the already mentioned "totally catastrophic collapse" and the "dreadful sensation of being ripped off or thrown away" (p. 170). Could this particular experience be compared to, or even sometimes actually repeat, that of a threatened miscarriage?

Mitrani may not have been far away from thinking along those lines herself, for in addition to seeing the breakdown of an "adhesive pseudo-object relationship" as the probable repetition of an early stage of development that had gone wrong (1996, p. 160), she allows for the possibility that this "aberration of normal development" might be "rooted in traumatic experiences of extreme deprivation occurring *in utero* [emphasis in original] and/or in early infancy" (p. 160); and she has also expressed an obvious interest in Mancia's 1981 paper on the mental life of the foetus. Mitrani's own interest in the possibility of reconstructing even pre- and perinatal body experiences came out even more strongly in her book *A Framework for the Imaginary* (1996; see, in particular, chapter 10, pp. 210–215, and yet another reference to Mancia's 1981 paper on pp. 232–233).

Speculating further still, Mitrani's reference to the absence of any "space" between subject and object in the "adhesive" type of relationship, as well as Ogden's concept of an "autistic–contiguous position", have given rise in my mind to the following thought. Total "contiguity" between the mother's womb and the unborn child can be said to have its strongest expression when the fertilized egg and early embryo are actually embedded in the uterine lining at the stage of "implantation". Eventually, however, the growing embryo loses this "absolute" contiguity by gradually detaching itself from the uterine wall at the end of a rapidly lengthening umbilical cord. The final "position" could therefore be described as follows: Despite the fact that a new "contiguity" will eventually re-establish itself between the foetus and the uterine wall as a result of the former having filled the whole of the womb's cavity, the initial and absolute contiguity that existed at implantation no longer exists: although still, of course, maintaining its "adhesion" to the uterine wall by means of its placenta, the foetal body proper has moved away from this wall at the end of the cord, and this means that a certain amount of "space" can now be said to exist between "subject" (foetal body) and "object" (mother). The separation from the mother at birth will, of course, result in an even greater "distance" or "space" between the two, although other forms of "adhesiveness", such as neediness and emotional clinging—or even of "contiguity" (physical handling, touching of skins etc.)—will continue for quite a while after, and indeed throughout life (adult relationships, love-making, search for physical and emotional contact, etc.). We are never quite as far removed from our earliest stages of development, therefore, as we may sometimes think.

There must be other works that could be said to have touched directly or indirectly on the possible relevance of prenatal life to postnatal psychology and behaviour. The future will, I think, lie in trying to see whether interpretations offered at prenatal level and within the transference in our everyday clinical work can really help our patients with their difficulties. We must not take it for granted that it will, although I can't help thinking that psychoanalysis might miss something by not at least attempting such research, and on a larger scale than has already been done by some of those mentioned here.

Before I conclude, however, I cannot resist the temptation of quoting two more of those works in which patients' unresolved prenatal cravings seem to have been successfully dealt with, even when the analyst had not directly referred to such cravings or offered the kind of interpretations just referred to.

A 1992 paper by O'Shaughnessy, for example, has warned against the possibility that difficulties with the countertransference may cause us either to take refuge in the "enclave" of some rigid theoretical framework, or else to let the patient step out of the analytic frame in some kind of extra-analytic "excursion". In quoting O'Shaughnessy's mention of this risk of the analyst taking refuge in theory, Mitrani, too, has shown her awareness of both these risks, but she has also wondered whether an "excursion" out of the analytic frame could sometimes become a useful experience for both patient and analyst (1996, p. 261). The context, as well as an examination of our countertransference, will probably help us to decide what to allow or not allow—as will a close examination of the transference. Regarding the latter, and in keeping with my chosen theme, I was interested in the dream of a patient reported by O'Shaughnessy (1992, p. 606). As O'Shaughnessy suggested, the "cracked . . . glass cloches" that the patient (Mrs B) had been supplied with in the dream had probably symbolized what seemed to have been the patient's fear of causing her analyst to "crack" (p. 607). If one takes into consideration the protective and growth-promoting function of "glass cloches" when used in gardening, could one also evoke the protective and growth-promoting function of the womb? In a later session, the patient had tried to persuade O'Shaughnessy to leave the consulting-room and take a walk out "in the sunshine" with her, which O'Shaughnessy interpreted as the patient's unconscious attempt to test the solidity of the "glass cloches" of the analytic stance. If I am right about the possible "womb" analogy, could one add that the patient had also unconsciously tried to test the solidity and quality of O'Shaughnessy's analytic "womb" to see whether it would "crack" under the pressure put on the latter by Mrs B's pressure to be allowed out of it—a pressure that, had it succeeded, would no doubt have confirmed her fear of being able to cause the analyst to "crack".

As I said when presenting and discussing my Patient A's treatment, we ourselves (the nurses and I on the first occasion and I alone on another) had not been able to contain the pressure of the anxieties that Miss A had aroused in us, and we had had to "terminate" the therapy and refer her back to the hospital that had sent her to us in the first place. In other words, the pressure put on us by what I took to be my patient's unresolved foetal cravings and aggressivity had made us feel that it would be too dangerous, both for Miss A and for all of us, to "hold" her any longer: we had "cracked". O'Shaughnessy's "womb", however, had not. The "excursion" out of the consulting-room—that is, the walk in the sun, which, the patient had said, would help, did not prove necessary: the analytic stance was maintained, and the patient had felt relieved (p. 607).

The second paper I wish to mention is an important one on paranoia by A. Cooper (1993). It did not *directly* suggest the possible role played in the formation of paranoid traits by unresolved prenatal cravings, but perhaps I can mention what makes me think that this paper, too, may have shown an intuitive awareness of that particular possibility. Returning once again to my Patient A, she had shown many instances of feeling persecuted by the world and the people in it. She had told me in her first session that almost within minutes of going through the hospital front door on admission, she had felt that "everyone had got it in" for her; and she had later described how the nurses, soon after her second admission, were forming a "circle" around her to "squeeze" both her and me out of the hospital. Although, as in the case of the patients alluded to by Cooper (1993, p. 429), such feelings could be explained in

Miss A's case by the presence of unresolved oral strivings, the obstetrical kind of language she had used to describe a "circle" that was "bearing down" on her had made me postulate the existence of an earlier pre/or perinatal kind of trauma, especially when she had began to say that even in her cocoon, where she had hoped to find safety, "death" was now trying to "get" her. I was therefore particularly interested to see that Cooper began this paper with a long extract from one of Kafka's "stories" ("The Burrow", 1923) and presented it as a "vivid description of the characteristics of the paranoid personality" (p. 423). Kafka's description of how his hero constructs and organizes an underground world to protect himself against intruders and Cooper's description of how this man, in the story, eventually "experiences the collapse of his defences" made me naturally think once again of how Miss A had hoped to find, in the "underground" world of her "prenatal" cocoon, a refuge against anyone who might try to "get" her, and of how this hope, too, had eventually "collapsed". Cooper's interest in that story thus seems to me to allow for the thought that he himself, even without referring to unresolved prenatal cravings, may have given us some reason for thinking that the persistence of such cravings might contribute to the formation of a "paranoid personality".

One last word, which may serve as some kind of conclusion to the present work as a whole. My misgivings about whether such work might be considered too "biological" and "deterministic" were considerably lessened by some articles that appeared in the *Bulletin of the British Psycho-Analytical Society* in the course of 2001 (especially in *Vol. 37*, No. 5; see also Symington, 2001). They show that psychoanalysis has not lost sight of what had been Freud's hope of increasing our understanding of how the psyche can develop out of its biological origins. The work of Kaplan-Solms and Solms, for example (2000, pp. 24–32, Solms, 2001), as well as the amount of thought that Fonagy is devoting to heredity, both give an idea of what can be done in this respect.

At the end of chapter four I suggested that analysts may eventually become interested in whether even genetic events and factors can sometimes be unwittingly referred to in the material of our patients. Should future research on those lines prove encouraging, this may then make it possible to identify in such material, and in its interaction with the "environment" of the analyst's countertransference, something that would this time have to be referred to as a *genetic* "theme"—one that would thus be deemed to accompany or underscore, like some kind of "counterpoint" or base-line, the prenatal theme with which the present work has mainly been concerned. Freud, rightly or wrongly, had been quite optimistic about the possibility of such developments eventually taking place in what he always liked to think of as our psychoanalytic "science". Others have not shared this view, but the future may be able to provide an answer.

NOTES

1. Dr Paul has very kindly let me know that at the top of column two of page 12 of his 1989 paper on "Mental Pressure", there is a publishing error that had not been noticed at the time: what is presented as a quotation from a paper by Dr Piontelli is, in fact, the reproduction of an extract from one of Paul's early works.

2. Analysts and therapists interested in prenatal "psychology" will find an extremely useful list of other references at the end of that last chapter of DeMause's 1982 book.

3. This allusion to Mason's paper was made in connection with Paul's own thoughts concerning a "penitential" type of transference that would be the result of what he too appears to conceive as a "crushing" and surrounding type of superego, and one moreover that he feels, as I do myself, may well have its origin in a persecutory experience of being "surrounded" and/or "suffocated" by the prenatal mother during labour. Since Mason's 1983 paper (as well as the earlier version of it which had already been published in 1981 by Caesura Press) had referred to Melanie Klein's description of the feeling of being imprisoned within the inside of the mother's body, he, too, could be said to have suggested the possibility of making a link between the concept of the "surrounding", "suffocating", "crushing" superego and the likewise surrounding and possibly crushing and suffocating birth-giving mother.

4. The word "dynamic", in this image of a "highly dynamic membrane" reminds me a little of the point that Elmhirst made when referring to the "container" (the maternal breast, according to Bion) as being by no means "static" (1983, p. 88).

5. My referring to the conceivability of "proto-psychological" exchanges taking place between mother and unborn child is, of course, another way of alluding to Bion's speculations about the foetus having some kind of "intelligence" (1980, p. 22), as well as to the possibility that states of mind in the pregnant mother might be capable of communicating themselves to the child inside her.

6. *The Skin-Ego* (1989) was translated into English from the French *Le Moi-Peau* (1985). I apologize for not having been able to check the English translation for the corresponding pages.

7. I gather from Pines's 1992 paper that the term "biological mirroring" had been used before (p. 24), but I do not know whether this had been by one of the authors, such as Emde and some others, whom he mentions a few lines earlier. Emde mentioned "mirroring" in the second part of a 1988 paper (p. 288); the term "biological mirroring" was not used then, but it is obvious from the whole of his paper that Emde sees biology as having an important contribution to make to psychoanalytic "science", and this without prejudice to the more human and "humanistic" aspects of psychoanalysis as a means of helping people with psychological difficulties (p. 293).

8. Balint had already tried, as far back as 1935, to identify an early stage of extra-uterine life that would precede the paranoid–schizoid position described by Melanie Klein, but the proposals put forward by Ogden on the one hand and Mitrani on the other concerning what they, too, feel could be a state that would antedate the paranoid–schizoid "position" are notably different from Balint's own proposals about what he called the stage of "primary object-love" (see also Melanie Klein, 1952a, pp. 198–236).

9. While appreciating (as I do myself), the "great value of Ogden's concept of the "autistic–contiguous position", Cruz Roche (1992, p. 363) has drawn attention to the fact that as long ago as 1962 and 1967, the Argentinian analyst J. Bleger had already proposed what he (Cruz Roche) describes as a similar concept or "position". The connotations of "stickiness", "viscosity", and "agglutination" suggested by the two Greek-derived words used by Bleger to describe the "position" postulated by him would, rather, seem to me, however, to evoke the "adhesive" type of identification identified by Bick (1968) and further studied by Meltzer (1975). I take up this point again below).

10. See again in this connection the importance attached to "skin" experiences by Anzieu (1989, 1990), Bick (1968), and several others; and also Mott's own remarks about the role he ascribed to the foetal skin in subsequent development (1964, pp. 43–90). Ogden himself has evoked "skin" sensations when describing the imitative type of relatedness often associated with the autistic–contiguous position (1989b, p. 136).

11. It is impossible for me to mention all the authors who have been interested in trying to get some idea of the nature of these very early and primitive forms of experience and relatedness. For a few more names that I have not included here, see Ogden, 1989b, p. 127, as well as Mitrani, 1995a, 1995b.

12. Maiello herself (1997, pp. 11, 15), had envisaged the possibility of conceiving Ogden's "autistic–contiguous position" as the continuation in postnatal life of some aspects of what one could call the prenatal "position".

REFERENCES

Abraham, K. (1913). Restrictions and transformations of scoptophilia in psycho-neurotics, with remarks on analogous phenomena in folk psychology. In: *Selected Papers* (pp. 169–234). London: Hogarth, 1942.
Abraham, K. (1922). The spider as a dream symbol. In: *Selected Papers* (pp. 326–332). London: Hogarth, 1942.
Adler, G. (1974). Regression in psychotherapy: Disruptive or therapeutic? *International Journal of Psychoanalytic Psychotherapy*, 3: 352–364.
Ammon, G. (1974). Vorgeburtliche Phantasien und Träume im Gruppenanalytischen Prozess. In: G. H. Graber (Ed.), *Pränatale Psychologie* (pp. 43–67). Munich: Kindler Verlag.
Anzieu, D. (1974). Le travail psychanalytique dans les groupes larges. *Bulletin de Psychologie* (Special Issue): 87–97.
Anzieu, D. (1985). *Le moi-peau*. Paris: Dunod.
Anzieu, D. (1989). *The Skin-Ego*. New Haven, CT: Yale University Press.
Anzieu, D. (1990). *Psychic Envelopes*. London: Karnac.
Aray, C., & Bellagamba, H. F. (1971). Observaciones sobra el fenómeno del doble en la situación analítica de un pacienta homosexual. In: A. Rascovsky et al., *Niveles profundos del psiquismo* (pp. 146–166). Buenos Aires: Editorial Sudamerica.
Balint, A. (1939). Love for the mother and mother love. In: *Primary Love and Psychoanalytic Technique* (pp. 109–127). London: Hogarth, 1952.
Balint, M. (1935). Critical notes on the pregenital organizations of the libido. In: *Primary Love and Psychoanalytic Technique* (pp. 49–12). London: Hogarth, 1952.
Balint, M. (1937). Early developmental states of the ego: Primary object love. In: *Primary Love and Psychoanalytic Technique* (pp. 90–108). London: Hogarth, 1952.

Balint, M. (1951). On love and hate. In: *Primary Love and Psychoanalytic Technique* (pp. 141–156). London: Hogarth, 1952.
Balint, M. (1952). New beginning and the paranoid and depressive syndromes. In: *Primary Love and Psychoanalytic Technique* (pp. 244–265). London: Hogarth, 1952.
Balint, M. (1968). *The Basic Fault: Therapeutic Aspects of Regression*. London: Tavistock.
Bick, E. (1968). The experience of the skin in early object relations. *International Journal of Psycho-Analysis, 49*: 484–486.
Bion, W. R. (1953). Notes on the theory of schizophrenia. In: *Second Thoughts* (pp. 23–35). New York: Jason Aronson, 1967.
Bion, W. R. (1956). Development of schizophrenic thought. In: *Second Thoughts* (pp. 36–42). New York: Jason Aronson, 1967.
Bion, W. R. (1957). Differentiation of the psychotic from the non-psychotic personalities. In: *Second Thoughts* (pp. 43–64). New York: Jason Aronson, 1967.
Bion, W. R. (1959). Attacks on linking. In: *Second Thoughts* (pp. 93–109). New York: Jason Aronson, 1967.
Bion, W. R. (1962). *Learning from Experience*. London: Heinemann.
Bion, W. R. (1963). *Elements of Psycho-Analysis*. London: Heinemann.
Bion, W. R. (1965). *Transformations*. London: Heinemann.
Bion, W. R. (1980). *Bion in New York and São Paulo*, ed. F. Bion. Strath Tay, Perthshire: Clunie Press.
Blarer, S. (1973). Der fötale Psychismus bei Rascovsky, Garma und Liley. In: G. H. Graber & F. Kruse (Eds.), *Vorgeburtliches Seelenleben* (pp. 82–97). Munich: W. Goldmann Verlag.
Blomfield, O. H. D. (1985). Parasitism, projective identification and the Faustian bargain. *International Review of Psycho-Analysis, 12*: 299–310.
Blomfield, O. H. D. (1987). Human destructiveness: An essay on instinct, foetal existence and infancy. *International Review of Psycho-Analysis, 14*: 21–32.
Bonaparte, M. (1936). Some paleobiological and biopsychical reflections. *International Journal of Psycho-Analysis, 19*, 1938: 214–220. (Original French publication: Vues paléobiologiques et biopsychiques. *Revue Française de Psychanalyse, 19*: 422–429.)
Bowlby, J. (1958). The nature of the child's tie to his mother. *International Journal of Psycho-Analysis, 39*: 350–373.
Brownscombe Heller, M. (1989). Dream work in psychoanalytic therapy. *British Journal of Psychotherapy, 6* (2): 154–159.
Bryce Boyer, L. B. (1978). Countertransference experiences with severely regressed patients. *Contemporary Psychoanalysis, 14*: 48–72.

Burger-Piaget, M. (1973). Observations cliniques de regressions foetales: Impulsions au suicide et incidences contretransférentielles. *Dynamische Psychiatrie, 20*: 117–198.

Caruso, I. A. (1973). Die Bedeutung des pränatalen Seelenlebens für die Persönlichkeitsentwicklung. In: G. H. Graber & F. Kruse (Eds.), *Vorgeburtliches Seelenleben* (pp. 65–72). Munich: W. Goldmann Verlag.

Chasseguet-Smirgel, J. (1984a). The femininity of the analyst in professional practice. *International Journal of Psycho-Analysis, 65*: 169–178.

Chasseguet-Smirgel, J. (1984b). The archaic matrix of the Oedipus complex. In: *Sexuality and Mind* (pp. 79–91). New York: New York University Press.

Chasseguet-Smirgel, J. (1990). On acting out. *International Journal of Psycho-Analysis, 71*: 77–86.

Chasseguet-Smirgel, J. (1992). Some thoughts on the psychoanalytic situation. *Journal of the American Psychoanalytic Association, 40*: 3–25.

Chiesa, M., & Fonagy, P. (2000). Cassel Hospital disorder study: Methodology and treatment effects. *British Journal of Psychiatry, 176*: 485–491.

Chiesa, M., & Fonagy, P. (2003). Psychosocial treatment for severe personality disorder: 36-month follow-up. *British Journal of Psychiatry*, 183 *(4)*: 356–362.

Cooper, A. M. (1993). Paranoia: A part of most analyses. *Journal of the American Psychoanalytic Association, 41* (2): 423–442.

Cruz-Roche, R. (1992). The autistic-contiguous position (Letter to the Editor). *International Journal of Psycho-Analysis, 73*: 363.

Davies, J. (1963). *Human Developmental Anatomy*. New York: Ronald Press.

DeMause, L. (1982). *Foundations of Psychohistory*. New York: Creative Roots.

Deutsch, H. (1942). Some forms of emotional disturbance and their relationship in schizophrenia. *Psychiatric Quarterly, 40*: 301–321.

Deutsch, H. (1947). *The Psychology of Women, Vol. 2*. London: Research Books.

Devereux, G. (1937). L'envoûtement chez les Indiens Mohaves. *Journal des Américanistes de Paris, 2* (29): 405–412.

Dolto, F. (1981a). *Au jeu du désir*. Paris: Seuil.

Dolto, F. (1981b). *La difficulté de vivre*. Paris: Interéditions.

Dowling, T. W. (1988). The use of placental symbols in assessing prenatal experience. In: P. G. Fedor-Freybergh & M. L. Vanessa Vogel (Eds.), *Prenatal and Perinatal Psychology and Medicine* (pp. 535–548). London/New York: Parthenon.

Eichenberger, E. (1973). Zeugung, Geburtstrauma, nachgeburtliche Entwicklung und Tod in der Psychologie G. H. Grabers. In: G. H. Graber & F. Kruse (Eds.), *Vorgeburtliches Seelenleben* (pp. 73–81). Munich: W. Goldmann Verlag.

Eisenberg, L. (1986). Mindlessness and brainlessness in psychiatry. *British Journal of Psychiatry, 146*: 497–508.

Elmhirst, S. Isaacs (1983). Bion and babies. In: J. S. Grotstein (Ed.), *Do I Dare Disturb the Universe?* (corrected edition, pp. 83–91). London: Karnac. (First published Beverly Hills, CA: Caesura Press, 1981.)

Emde, R. (1988). Development terminable and interminable, Part II: Recent psychoanalytic theory and therapeutic considerations. *International Journal of Psycho-Analysis, 69*: 283–296.

Evans, G. (1955). Early anxiety situations in the analysis of a boy in the latency period. In: M. Klein, P. Heimann, & R. Money-Kyrle (Eds.), *New Directions in Psychoanalysis* (pp. 48–81). London: Tavistock. Reprinted London: Karnac, 1977.

Fedor-Freybergh, P. G., & Vogel, V. (1988). Introduction. In: *Prenatal and Perinatal Psychology and Medicine* (pp. xviii–xxxii). London/New York: Parthenon.

Fenichel, O. (1946). *The Psycho-Analytic Theory of Neurosis*. London: Kegan Paul, French, Trubner.

Ferenczi, S. (1913). Stages in the development of the sense of reality. In: *First Contributions to Psychoanalysis* (pp. 213–239). London: Hogarth, 1952.

Ferenczi, S. (1933). Thalassa: A theory of genitality (1). *Psychoanalytic Quarterly, 2*: 361.

Ferenczi, S. (1934). Thalassa: A theory of genitality (2). *Psychoanalytic Quarterly, 3*: 1.

Fodor, N. (1949). *The Search for the Beloved*. New York: University Books.

Fodor, N. (1951). *New Approaches to Dream Interpretation*. New York: International Universities Press.

Fodor, N. (1962). *Love, Birth, and Trauma*. New York: Citadel Press.

Fonagy, P. (2001). What does developmental psychopathology know about the mind? *The Bulletin of the British Psycho-Analytical Society, 37* (5): 10–17.

Fonagy, P. (2003). Genetics, developmental psycho-pathology, and psychoanalytic theory: The case for our ending our (not so) splendid isolation. *Psychoanalytic Inquiry, 23* (2): 218–247.

Foulkes, S. H. (1971). Dynamische Prozesse in der gruppenanalytischen Situation. In: A. Heigl-Evers (Ed.), *Psychoanalyse und Gruppen*. Göttingen: Vandenboeck und Ruprecht.

Freud, S. (1912b). The dynamics of transference. *SE, 12*, pp. 97–108.
Freud, S. (1915c). *Instincts and Their Vicissitudes. SE, 14*, pp. 111–140.
Freud, S. (1916–17). *Introductory Lectures on Psycho-Analysis. SE, 15–16*, pp. 149–169.
Freud, S. (1918b). From the history of an infantile neurosis. *SE, 19*, pp. 7–122.
Freud, S. (1920g). *Beyond the Pleasure Principle. SE, 18*, pp. 3–64.
Freud, S. (1923b). *The Ego and the Id. SE, 19*, pp. 3–66.
Freud, S. (1924). Letter to Abraham. In: *Ernest Jones: The Life and Work of Sigmund Freud*, ed. L. Trilling & S. Marcus. London: Pelican, 1964.
Freud, S. (1931b). Female sexuality. *SE, 21*: 223–243.
Freud, S. (1933a). *New Introductory Lectures on Psycho-Analysis*. London: Hogarth.
Freud, W. E. (1985). Prenatal attachment and bonding. In: *The Birth of a New Science*. Selected papers from the First Congress of Pre- and Perinatal Psychology, 1983, Toronto.
Freud, W. E. (1988a). The concept of cathexis and its usefulness for prenatal psychology. In: P. G. Fedor-Freybergh & M. L. Vanessa Vogel (Eds.), *Prenatal and Perinatal Psychology and Medicine* (pp. 165–175). London/New York: Parthenon.
Freud, W. E. (1988b). Prenatal attachment, the prenatal continuum, and the psychological side of neo-natal intensive care. In: P. G. Fedor-Freybergh & M. L. Vanessa Vogel (Eds.), *Prenatal and Perinatal Psychology and Medicine*. London/New York: Parthenon.
Freud, W. E. (1989). Prenatal attachment and bonding. In: S. Greenspan & G. Pollock (Eds.), *The Course of Life, Vol. I: Infancy* (pp. 467–483). Madison, CT: International Universities Press.
Frosh, S. (1990). Book review of *New Essays on Narcissism*, by B. Grunberger. *British Journal of Psychotherapy, 7* (2): 192–196.
Gaddini, E. (1969). On imitation. *International Journal of Psycho-Analysis, 50* (4): 475–484.
Garma, A. (1958). Interpretaciones en sueños del psiquismo fetal. *Revista de psicoanálisis, 15*.
Garma, A. (1966). *The Psychoanalysis of Dreams*. Chicago, IL: Quadrangle Books.
Garma, A. (1970). *Nuevas aportaciones al psicoanálisis de los sueños*. Buenos Aires: Paidos.
Garma, A. (1974). Das fötale Seelenleben und das Geburtstrauma im Ursprung aller Träume. In: G. H. Graber & F. Kruse (Eds.), *Pränatale Psychologie* (pp. 13–22). Munich: Kindler Verlag.
Gesell, A. (1945). *The Embryology of Behaviour*. New York: Harper & Row.

Giard, A. (1913). *Oeuvres diverses, 1911–1913* (2 vols.). Paris.
Glover, E. (1943). The concept of dissociation. *International Journal of Psycho-Analysis, 24:* 7–13.
Graber, G. H. (1924). Die Ambivalenz des Kindes. *Imago Buch No. VI.* Vienna: Internationale Psychoanalytische Verlag.
Graber, G. H. (1972). *Neue Beiträge zur Lehre und Praxis der Psychotherapie.* Munich: W. Goldmann Verlag.
Graber, G. H. (1973). Grundlagenforschung und Geschichte der Internationalen Studiengemeinschaft für Pränatale Psychologie. In: G. H. Graber & F. Kruse (Eds.), *Vorgeburtliches Seelenleben* (pp. 11–20). Munich: W. Goldmann Verlag.
Graber, G. H. (1975). *Gesammelte Schriften.* Munich: W. Goldmann Verlag.
Greenacre, P. (1941). The predisposition to anxiety. In: *Trauma, Growth and Personality* (pp. 3–24). London: Hogarth, 1953.
Greenacre, P. (1945). The biological economy of birth. In: *Trauma, Growth and Personality* (pp. 25–30). London: Hogarth, 1953.
Grof, S. (1976). *Realms of the Human Unconscious.* New York: E. P. Dutton.
Grof, S. (1983). *Topographie des Unbewussten.* Stuttgart: Klett-Cotta.
Grotstein, J. S. (1977a). The psychoanalytic concept of schizophrenia, I: The dilemma. *International Journal of Psycho-Analysis, 58:* 403–425.
Grotstein, J. S. (1977b). The psychoanalytic concept of schizophrenia, II: Reconciliation. *International Journal of Psycho-Analysis, 58:* 427–452.
Grotstein, J. S. (1978). Gradients in analysability. *International Journal of Psychoanalytic Psychotherapy, 7:* 137–151.
Grotstein, J. S. (1981). *Splitting and Projective Identification.* New York/ London: Jason Aronson.
Grotstein, J. S. (1983a). Who is the dreamer who dreams the dream? In: J. S. Grotstein (Ed.), *Do I Dare Disturb the Universe?* (corrected edition, pp. 358–416). London: Karnac. (First published Beverly Hills, CA: Caesura Press, 1981.)
Grotstein, J. S. (1983b). Book review of Tustin's *Autistic States in Children. International Review of Psycho-Analysis, 10:* 491–498.
Grunberger, B. (1983). Narcisse et Anubis. *Revue Française de Psychanalyse, 47:* 921–938.
Grunberger, B. (1989). *New Essays on Narcissism.* London: Free Association.
Guntrip, H. (1971). *Psychoanalytic Theory: Therapy and the Self.* New York: Basic Books.
Haesler, W. T. (1974). Die Strafanstalt: Ort der Zuflucht, Ort der Wandlung? In: G. H. Graber (Ed.), *Pränatale Psychologie* (pp. 88–96). Munich: Kindler Verlag.

REFERENCES 151

Hahn, R., & Kleinman, A. (1983). Belief as pathogen, belief as medicine: Voodoo death and "placebo phenomenon" in anthropological perspective. *Medical Anthropology, 14*: 6–19.

Hamilton, W. J., Boyd, J. D., & Mossman, H. W. (1945). *Human Embryology*. Cambridge: Heffer.

Hartmann, H. (1950). Comments on the psychoanalytic concept of the ego. In: *Essays on Ego-Psychology* (pp. 113–141). London: Hogarth, 1964.

Hartmann, H. (1956). Notes on the reality principle. In: *Essays on Ego-Psychology* (pp. 241–267). London: Hogarth, 1964.

Hau, T. (1973). Perinatale und pränatale Factoren der Neurosenätiologie. In: G. H. Graber & F. Kruse (Eds.), *Vorgeburtliches Seelenleben* (pp. 129–142). Munich: W. Goldmann Verlag.

Hau, T., & Schindler, S. (1982). *Narzismus und Intentionalität—prä- und perinatale Aspekte* (pp. 29–38). Stuttgart: Hippokrates Verlag.

Hepper, P. G. (1989). Foetal learning: Implications for psychiatry. *British Journal of Psychiatry, 155*: 289–293.

Hochmann, J. (1976). Les dents de la mère. *L'Evolution Psychiatrique, 41* (3): 619–661.

Hooker, D. (1952). *The Prenatal Origin of Behaviour*. Lawrence, KS: University of Kansas Press.

Hooker, D. (1964). The sequence in human fetal activity. In: C. B. Stendler (Ed.): *Readings in Child Behaviour and Development* (pp. 11–17). New York: Harcourt Brace.

Janus, L. (1986). *Vorgeburtliche Lebenszeit und Geburtserleben. Ein verborgenes Basisthema der Psychoanalyse*. Heidelberg: Bischoff.

Janus, L. (1988). The trauma of birth as reflected in the psychoanalytic process. In: P. G. Fedor-Freybergh & M. L. Vanessa Vogel (Eds.), *Prenatal and Perinatal Psychology and Medicine* (pp. 177–188). London/New York: Parthenon.

Janus, L. (1990). Fantasies of regression to the womb as central elements in the psychoanalytic process. *International Journal of Prenatal and Perinatal Studies*: 89–100.

Joffe, J. M. (1969). *Prenatal Determinants of Behaviour*. London/New York: Pergamon Press.

Joseph, B. (1982). Addiction to near death. *International Journal of Psychoanalysis, 63* (4): 449–456.

Joseph, B. (1983). Toward the experiencing of psychic pain. In: J. S. Grostein (Ed.), *Do I Dare Disturb the Universe?* (corrected edition, pp. 93–102). London: Karnac. (First published Beverly Hills, CA: Caesura Press, 1981.) Also in: E. B. Spillius & M. Feldman (Eds.), *Psychic Equilibrium and Psychic Change (Selected Papers of Betty Joseph)* (pp. 88–97). New York: Tavistock/Routledge, 1989.

Kaplan-Solms, K., & Solms, M. (2000). *Clinical Studies in Neuro-Psychoanalysis.* London: Karnac.

Kelsey, D. (1953). Phantasies of birth and prenatal experiences recovered from patients undergoing hypnoanalysis. *Journal of Mental Science,* 19: 216–233.

Khan, M. M. R. (1974). *The Privacy of the Self.* London: Hogarth.

Kind, P., Rosser, R., Williams, A. (1982). A valuation of quality of life: Some psychometric evidence. In: M. Jones-Lee (Ed.), *The Value of Life and Safety* (pp. 159–170). Amsterdam: North Holland.

Klein, M. (1932). *The Psycho-Analysis of Children* (2nd edition). London: Hogarth, 1937.

Klein, M. (1933). The early development of conscience in the child. In: *Contributions to Psycho-Analysis* (pp. 267–277). London: Hogarth, 1948.

Klein, M. (1945). The Oedipus complex in the light of early anxieties. In: *Contributions to Psycho-Analysis* (pp. 339–390). London: Hogarth, 1948.

Klein, M. (1946). Notes on some schizoid mechanisms. In: J. Riviere (Ed.), *Developments in Psycho-Analysis* (pp. 292—320). London: Hogarth, 1952.

Klein, M. (1948). On the theory of anxiety and guilt. In: J. Riviere (Ed.), *Developments in Psycho-Analysis* (pp. 270–291). London: Hogarth, 1952.

Klein, M. (1952a). On observing the behaviour of small infants. In: J. Riviere (Ed.), *Developments in Psycho-Analysis* (pp. 237–270). London: Hogarth.

Klein, M. (1952b). Some theoretical conclusions regarding the emotional life of the infant. In: J. Riviere (Ed.), *Developments in Psycho-Analysis* (pp. 198–236). London: Hogarth.

Klein, M. (1955). On identification. In: *New Directions in Psycho-Analysis* (pp. 309–345). London: Karnac.

Klein, M. (1957). Envy and gratitude. In: *Envy & Gratitude and Other Works* (pp. 176–235). London: Hogarth.

Klein, S. (1980). Autistic phenomena in neurotic patients. *International Journal of Psycho-Analysis,* 61: 395–402.

Klein, S. (1984). Delinquent perversion. Problems of assimilation: A clinical study. *International Journal of Psycho-Analysis,* 65: 307–314.

Kohut, H. (1971). *The Analysis of the Self.* New York: International Universities Press.

Kruse, F. (1969). *Die Anfänge des menschlichen Seelenlebens.* Stuttgart: Enke.

Kruse, F. (1973a). Der pränatale Mensch. *Imago Mundi,* 4: 141–168.

Kruse, F. (1973b). Die Anfänge der individuellen Erfahrungsbildung. In:

G. H. Graber & F. Kruse (Eds.), *Vorgeburtliches Seelenleben*. Munich: W. Goldmann Verlag.
Laibow, R. E. (1988). Prenatal and perinatal experiences and developmental impairment. In: P. G. Fedor-Freybergh & L. Vanessa Vogel (Eds.), *Prenatal and Perinatal Psychology and Medicine* (pp. 295-308). London/New York: Parthenon.
Laing, R. D. (1976). *The Facts of Life*. London: Allen Lane.
Lake, F. (1973). Summary of statements of patients who believed themselves to be experiencing the process of birth in the second stage of labor. *Energy and Character, 4* (1): 15-22.
Langman, R. J. (1969). *Medical Embryology*. Baltimore, MD: Williams & Wilkins.
Langs, R. J. (1976). *The Therapeutic Interaction, Vol. II*. New York: Jason Aronson.
Langs, R. J. (1978). Some communicative properties of the bipersonal field. *International Journal of Psychoanalytic Psychotherapy, 7*: 413-472.
Lawson, A. H. (1984). Perinatal imagery in UFO abduction reports. *Journal of Psychohistory, 12* (2): 213-239.
Lietaert Peerbolte, M. (1951). Psychotherapeutic evaluation of birth-trauma analysis. *Psychiatric Quarterly, 25*: 589-603.
Lietaert Peerbolte, M. (1952). Some problems connected with Fodor's birth-trauma therapy. *Psychiatric Quarterly, 26*: 264-305.
Lietaert Peerbolte, M. (1975). *Psychic Energy*. Wassenaar: Servire Publishers.
Liley, A. W. (1967). The foetus in control of his environment. In: *Montgomery Spencer Memorial Oration*, RALP.
Liley, A. W. (1972). The foetus as a personality. *Australian and New Zealand Journal of Psychiatry, 6*: 99-105.
Little, M. (1960). On basic unity. *International Journal of Psycho-Analysis, 41*: 377-384.
Little, M. (1966). Transference in borderline states. *International Journal of Psycho-Analysis, 47*: 476-485.
Mahler, M. (1952). On child psychosis and schizophrenia: Autistic and symbiotic infantile psychoses. *Psychoanalytic Study of the Child, 7*: 286-305.
Mahler, M. (1967). On human symbiosis and the vicissitudes of individuation. *Journal of the American Psychoanalytic Association, 15*: 740-763.
Mahler, M. (1971). Disturbances of symbiosis and individuation in the development of the psychotic ego. In: P. Doucet & C. Laurin (Eds.), *Problems of Psychosis* (pp. 188-195). Amsterdam: Excerpta Medica, International Congress Series.

Mahler, M., Pine, F., & Bergman, A. (1975). *The Psychological Birth of the Human Infant: Symbiosis and Individuation*: New York: Basic Books.
Maiello, S. (1995). The sound object. *Journal of Child Psychotherapy*, 21: 23–41. (First published as "L'Ogetto Sonoro", Richard e Piggle, 1, 1993: 31–47.)
Maiello, S. (1997). Going beyond: Notes on the beginning of object relations in the light of "The perpetuation of an error". In: T. Mitrani & J. Mitrani (Eds.), *Encounters with Autistic States: A Memorial Tribute to Frances Tustin* (pp. 1–22). Northvale, NJ/London: Jason Aronson.
Maiello, S. (2001). Prenatal trauma and autism. *Journal of Child Psychotherapy*, 27 (2): 107–124.
Maizels, N. (1985). Self-envy, the womb, and the nature of goodness: A reappraisal of the death instinct. *International Journal of Psycho-Analysis*, 66: 185–192.
Mancia, M. (1981). On the beginning of mental life in the foetus. *International Journal of Psycho-Analysis*, 62 (3): 351–357.
Mason, A. A. (1981). The suffocating superego: Psychotic break and claustrophobia. In: J. S. Grotstein (Ed.), *Do I Dare Disturb the Universe?* (corrected edition, pp. 139–166). London: Karnac. (First published Beverly Hills, CA: Caesura Press, 1981.)
Meltzer, D. (1963a). Contribution to the metapsychology of cyclothymic states. In: A. Hahn (Ed.), *Sincerity and Other Works: Collected Papers by Donald Meltzer*. London: Karnac, 1994.
Meltzer, D. (1963b). The differentiation of somatic delusions from hypochondria. In: A. Hahn (Ed.), *Sincerity and Other Works: Collected Papers by Donald Meltzer*. London: Karnac, 1994.
Meltzer, D. (1967). *The Psycho-Analytic Process*. London: William Heinemann Medical Books.
Meltzer, D. (1974). Mutism in infantile autism, schizophrenia, and manic depressive states. *International Journal of Psycho-Analysis*, 55: 397–404.
Meltzer, D. (1975). Adhesive identification. *Contemporary Psychoanalysis*, 11: 289–310.
Meltzer, D. (1978). *The Kleinian Development, Vol. III: The Clinical Significance of the Work of Bion*. Strath Tay, Perthshire: Clunie Press.
Meltzer, D. (1986). *Studies in Extended Metapsychology*. Strath Tay, Perthshire: Clunie Press.
Meltzer, D., & Harris Williams, M. (1988). The aesthetic conflict. In: *The Apprehension of Beauty: The Role of the Aesthetic Conflict in Development, Violence, and Art* (pp. 7–33). Strath Tay, Perthshire: Clunie Press.
Meltzer, D., & Harris Williams, M. (2001). The story of child develop-

ment: A psychoanalytic account. *Infant Observation (International Journal of Infant Observation and Its Applications)*, 4 (2): 36–50.
Menninger, K. A. (1939). An anthropological note on the theory of prenatal instinctual conflict. *International Journal of Psycho-Analysis*, 20: 439–442.
Milaković, I. (1967). The hypothesis of a deglutitive phase in libidinal development. *International Journal of Psycho-Analysis*, 48: 76–82.
Milaković, I. (1982). Pränatale Adaptation Prozesse und ihre psychophysischen Grundlagen. In: T. F. Hau & S. Schindler (Eds.), *Pränatale und perinatale Psychosomatik* (pp. 124–131). Stuttgart: Hippokrates Verlag.
Mitrani, J. (1993). Deficiency and envy: Some factors impacting the analytic mind from listening to interpretation. *International Journal of Psycho-Analysis*, 74 (4): 689–704.
Mitrani, J. (1994). On adhesive pseudo-object relations: Part 1—theory. *Contemporary Psychoanalysis*, 30 (2): 348–366.
Mitrani, J. (1995a). On adhesive pseudo-object relations: An illustration. In: *A Framework for the Imaginary* (pp. 171–203). Northvale, NJ/London: Jason Aronson.
Mitrani, J. (1995b). Toward an understanding of unmentalized experience. In: *A Framework for the Imaginary* (pp. 205–247). Northvale, NJ/London: Jason Aronson.
Mitrani, J. (1996). *A Framework for the Imaginary*. Northvale, NJ/London: Jason Aronson.
Modell, A. H. (1976). The holding environment and the therapeutic action of psychoanalysis. *Journal of the American Psychoanalytic Association*, 24: 285–307.
Modell, A. H. (1984). *Psychoanalysis in a New Context*. New York: International Universities Press.
Money-Kyrle, R. (1968). Cognitive development. *International Journal of Psycho-Analysis*, 49: 691–698.
Montagu, A. (1964). *Life Before Birth*. London: Longmans.
Mott, F. J. (1948). *The Universal Design of Birth*. Philadelphia, PA: David McKay.
Mott, F. J. (1959). *The Nature of the Self*. London: Allen Wingate.
Mott, F. J. (1960). *Mythology and the Prenatal Life*. London: Integration Publishing Company.
Mott, F. J. (1964). *The Universal Design of Creation*. Edenbridge: Mark Beech Publishers.
Ogden, T. H. (1982). *Projective Identification and Psychotherapeutic Technique*. New York: Jason Aronson.
Ogden, T. H. (1988). On the dialectical structure of experience: Some

clinical and theoretical implications. *Contemporary Psychoanalysis, 23*: 17–45.

Ogden, T. H. (1989a). *The Primitive Edge of Experience*. Northvale, NJ/London: Jason Aronson.

Ogden, T. H. (1989b). The autistic–contiguous position. *International Journal of Psycho-Analysis, 70* (1): 127–146.

O'Shaughnessy, E. (1992). Enclaves and excursions. *International Journal of Psycho-Analysis, 73*: 603–611.

Osterweil, E. (1990). "A Psychoanalytic Exploration of Fetal Mental Development and Its Role in the Origin of Object Relations." Doctoral Dissertation, California Graduate Institute, Los Angeles.

Page, E. W. (1963). Functions of the human placenta. *Modern Medicine* (Special article, February): 143–153.

Paul, M. I. (1983). A mental atlas of the process of psychological birth. In: J. Grotstein (Ed.), *Do I Dare Disturb the Universe?* (corrected edition, pp. 552–570). London: Karnac. (First published Beverly Hills, CA: Caesura Press, 1981.)

Paul, M. I. (1989). Notes on the primordial development of the penitential transference. *Melanie Klein and Object Relations, 7* (2): 43–69.

Paul, M. I. (1990). Studies on the phenomenology of mental pressure. *Melanie Klein and Object Relations, 8* (2): 1–20.

Pierce Clark, L. (1933). *The Nature and Treatment of Amentia*. Baltimore, MD: William Wood.

Pines, M. (1984). Reflections on mirroring. *International Review of Psycho-Analysis, 11*: 27–42.

Pines, M. (1992). Eduardo Cortesão: An appreciation. *British Psycho-Analytical Society Bulletin, 28* (2): 20–28.

Piontelli, A. (1987). Infant observation before birth. *International Journal of Psycho-Analysis, 68*: 453–463.

Piontelli, A. (1988). Prenatal life and birth as reflected in the analysis of a two-year old psychotic girl. *International Review of Psycho-Analysis, 15*: 73–81.

Piontelli, A. (1992). *From Foetus to Child*. London: Routledge.

Piontelli, A. (2002). *Twins: From Fetus to Child*. London & New York: Routledge.

Ployé, P. M. (1973). Does prenatal mental life exist? *International Journal of Psycho-Analysis, 54*: 241–246. (French: Existe-t-il un psychisme prénatal? *Evolution Psychiatrique, 41*, 1976: 663–675.)

Ployé, P. M. (1977). On some difficulties of inpatient, individual, psychoanalytically oriented therapy. *Psychiatry, 40*: 133–145. (German: Über einige Schwierigkeiten bei der psychoanalytisch orientierten Einzeltherapie von Klinikpatienten. In: *Psychotherapie in der Klinik* (pp. 183–204). Berlin/Heidelberg/New York: Springer-Verlag.)

Ployé, P. M. (1984). A note on two important aspects of Kleinian theory: "Projective identification" and "idealization". *British Journal of Psychiatry, 145*: 55–58.
Rank, O. (1914). Der Doppelgänger. *Imago, 13*.
Rank, O. (1924). *The Trauma of Birth.* New York: Robert Brunner, 1952.
Raphael-Leff, J. (1992). Relationship across the divide: Effects of perinatal conceptualisations on perinatal encounters. *British Psycho-Analytical Society Bulletin, 28* (5): 1–15.
Rascovsky, A. (1956). Beyond the oral stage. *International Journal of Psycho-Analysis, 37*: 286–289.
Rascovsky, A., & Rascovsky, M. (1971a). Significado, profundida y alcance de la regressión en la manía. In: *Niveles Profundos del Psiquismo* (pp. 11–59). Buenos Aires: Editorial Sudamericana.
Rascovsky, A., et al. (1971b). Consideraciones sobre la transferencia/contratransferencia en los estados maníacos. In: *Niveles Profundos del Psiquismo* (pp. 167–192). Buenos Aires: Editorial Sudamericana.
Roheim, G. (1952). *The Gates of the Dream.* New York: International Universities Press.
Rosenfeld, H. (1947). Analysis of a schizophrenic state in depersonalisation. In: *Psychotic States* (pp. 13–33). London: Hogarth, 1965.
Rosenfeld, H. (1950). Notes on the psychopathology of confusional states in chronic schizophrenia. In: *Psychotic States: A Psychoanalytic Approach* (pp. 63–103). London: Hogarth, 1965.
Rosenfeld, H. (1952a). Notes on the psychoanalysis of the superego conflict in an acute catatonic schizophrenic patient. In: *Psychotic States: A Psychoanalytic Approach* (pp. 155–168). London: Hogarth, 1965.
Rosenfeld, H. (1952b). Transference phenomena and transference analysis in an acute schizophrenic patient. In: *Psychotic States* (pp. 104–116). London: Hogarth, 1965.
Rosenfeld, H. (1965). *Psychotic States: A Psychoanalytic Approach.* New York: International Universities Press.
Rosenfeld, H. (1971). Contribution to the psychopathology of psychotic states: The importance of projective identification in the ego-structure and the object relations of the psychotic patient. In: P. Doucet & C. Laurin (Eds.), *Problems of Psychosis.* Amsterdam: Excerpta Medica, International Congress Series.
Rosenfeld, H. (1983). Primitive objective relations and mechanisms. *International Journal of Psycho-Analysis, 64*: 261–267.
Rosenfeld, H. (1987). *Impasse and Interpretation. The New Library of Psychoanalysis, No. 1,* ed. D. Tuckett. New York/London: Tavistock & The Institute of Psycho-Analysis.
Rowan, J. (1991). Comment on Robert Whyte's paper "Giving and taking". *British Journal of Psychotherapy, 8* (2): 206–207.

Rucker, N. (1994). Reflecting on prenatal experience in psychoanalytic imagery, motifs and process. *British Journal of Psychotherapy*, 11: 209–220.
Rushton, D. I. (1973). The placenta: An environmental problem. *British Medical Journal* (10 February): 344–348.
Sarkissoff, J. (1974). Die Nützung der fötalen mutterlichen Stimme (nach Tomatis) in der Psychotherapie. In: G. H. Graber (Ed.), *Pränatale Psychologie* (pp. 122–126). Munich: Kindler Verlag.
Schindler, S. (1973). Methoden der peri- und pränatalen Psychologie. In: G. H. Graber & F. Kruse (Eds.), *Vorgeburtliches Seelenleben* (pp. 98–105). Munich: W. Goldmann Verlag.
Schindler, S. (1975). Die Bedeutung der pränatalen Psychologie für die Entwicklung. *Vortrag 3 Tagungs der ISPP.* Munich: Weidenkam.
Schindler, S. (1982a). Der träumende Fetus. In: T. F. Hau & S. Schindler (Eds.), *Pränatale und Perinatale Psychosomatik* (pp. 111–118). Stuttgart: Hippokrates Verlag.
Schindler, S. (1982b). Wo bin ich? Zur Situation des Geborenwerdens. In: S. Schindler (Ed.), *Geburt: Eintritt in eine neue Welt* (pp. 17–25). Göttingen/Toronto/Zurich: Verlag für Psychologie.
Schindler, S. (1988). A new view of the unborn: Toward a developmental psychology of the prenatal period. In: P. G. Freybergh & M. L. Vanessa Vogel (Ed.), *Prenatal and Perinatal Psychology and Medicine* (pp. 23–33). London/New York: Parthenon.
Schusser, G. (1988). The connection between the course of pregnancy and postnatal mother–child interaction. In: P. G. Fedor-Freybergh & M. L. Vanessa Vogel (Eds.), *Prenatal and Perinatal Psychology and Medicine* (pp. 35–51). London/New York: Parthenon.
Scott, W. C. M. (1949). The body scheme in psychotherapy. *British Journal of Medical Psychology*, 22 (3–4): 144.
Searles, H. (1965). *Collected Papers on Schizophrenia and Related Subjects*. New York: International Universities Press.
Segal, H. (1950). Some aspects of the analysis of a schizophrenic. *International Journal of Psycho-Analysis*, 31: 268–278.
Segal, H. (1956). Depression in the schizophrenic. *International Journal of Psycho-Analysis*, 37: 339–343.
Segal, H. (1957). Notes on symbol formation. *International Journal of Psycho-Analysis*, 38: 391–397.
Segal, H. (1981). *The Work of Hanna Segal*. New York: Jason Aronson.
Segal, H. (1983). Some clinical implications of Melanie Klein's work: Emergence from narcissism. *International Journal of Psycho-Analysis*, 64: 269–276.
Share, L. (1992). "Birth and Infant Trauma as Reconstructed from

Dreams and Lived Out in the Character." Doctoral dissertation, Psychoanalytic Centre of California.

Share, L. (1994). *If Someone Speaks It Gets Lighter: Dreams and the Reconstruction of Infant Trauma.* Mahwah, NJ: Analytic Press.

Simmel, E. (1929). Psycho-analytic treatment of patients in a sanatorium. *International Journal of Psycho-Analysis, 10*: 70–89.

Sohn, L. (1985). Narcissistic organization, projective identification, and the formation of the identificate. *International Journal of Psycho-Analysis, 66*: 203–213.

Solms, M. (2001). An example of neuro-psychoanalytic research: Korsakoff's syndrome. *Bulletin of the British Psycho-Analytical Society, 37* (5): 24–32.

Sontag, L. W. (1940). Effect of fetal activity on the nutritive state of the infant at birth. *American Journal of Diseases in Children, 60*: 621–630.

Sontag, L. W. (1941). The significance of fetal environmental differences. *American Journal of Obstetrics and Gynaecology, 42*: 996–1003.

Sontag, L. W. (1944). Differences in modifiability of fetal behaviour and psychology. *Psychosomatic Medicine, 6*: 151–154.

Sontag, L. W. (1966). Implications of fetal behaviour and environment for adult personalities. *Annals of the New York Academy of Sciences, 134*: 782–786.

Spillius, E. Bott (1993). Varieties of envious experience. *International Journal of Psychoanalysis, 74*: 1199–1212.

Steiner, R. (1999). Some notes on the "heroic self" and the meaning and importance of its reparation for the creative process and the creative personality. *International Journal of Psycho-Analysis, 80*: 685–718.

Symington, J. (1988). The analysis of a mentally handicapped youth. *International Review of Psycho-Analysis, 15*: 243–250.

Symington, N. (1981). The psychotherapy of a subnormal patient. *British Journal of Psychology, 54*: 167–199.

Symington, N. (1983). The analyst's act of freedom as agent of therapeutic change. *International Review of Psycho-Analysis, 10*: 283–291.

Symington, N. (1993). *Narcissism: A New Theory.* London: Karnac.

Symington, N. (2001). Models of the mind. *Bulletin of the British Psycho-Analytical Society, 37* (5): 63–64.

This, B. (1960). *La Psychanalyse.* Paris: Casterman.

Tustin, F. (1981). *Autistic States in Children.* London: Hogarth.

Tustin, F. (1983). Psychological birth and psychological catastrophe. In: J. Grotstein (Ed.), *Do I Dare Disturb the Universe?* (corrected edition, pp. 181–196). London: Karnac. (First published Beverly Hills, CA: Caesura Press, 1981.)

Tustin, F. (1986). *Autistic Barriers in Neurotic Patients.* London: Karnac.

Tustin, F. (1991). Revised understanding of psychogenic autism. *International Journal of Psycho-Analysis*, 72: 585–591.
Van Den Bergh B. R. H. (1988). The relationship between maternal emotionality during pregnancy and the behavioural development of the foetus and neonate. In: P. G. Fedor-Freybergh & M. L. Vanessa Vogel (Eds.), *Prenatal and Perinatal Psychology and Medicine* (pp. 131–142). London/New York: Parthenon.
Verny, T. (1981). *The Secret Life of the Unborn Child*. New York: Summit Books. Reprinted London: Sphere, 1982.
Veszy-Wagner, L. (1966). The analyst provides a new cushion. *British Psycho-Analytical Society Bulletin*, 4: 13–16.
Whyte, R. (1991). Giving and taking: The foetal–maternal placental junction as a prototype and precursor of object relations. *British Journal of Psychotherapy*, 7: 221–229.
Wilheim, J. (1988). *A Caminho do Nascimento—Uma ponte entre o biológico e o psíquico* (pp. 52–95). São Paulo: Imago Editora. (German: *Unterwegs zur Geburt*. Heidelberg: Mattes, 1995.)
Winick, M. (1983). Fetal malnutrition and brain development. *Journal of Pediatric Gastroenterology and Nutrition*, 2 (Suppl. 1): S68–S72.
Winnicott, D. W. (1949). Birth memories, birth trauma and anxiety. In: *Collected Papers: Through Paediatrics to Psycho-Analysis*. London: Tavistock, 1958.
Winnicott, D. W. (1960). The theory of the infant–parent relationship. *International Journal of Psycho-Analysis*, 41: 585–595.
Winnicott, D. W. (1965). *The Maturational Processes and the Facilitating Environment*. New York: International Universities Press.
Winnicott, D. W. (1967). Mirror-role of mother and family in child development. In: *Playing and Reality* (pp. 111–118). London: Tavistock.
Wright, K. (1991). *Vision and Separation: Between Mother and Baby*. London: Free Association.
Yorke, C. (1988). A defect in training. *British Journal of Psychiatry*, 152: 159–164.
Yorke, C. (1994). Freud or Klein? *International Journal of Psycho-Analysis*, 75: 375–385.

INDEX

abortion attempts, 15
Abraham, K., 5, 37
ABREP (Brazilian Association for the Study of Pre- and Perinatal Psychism), 6
acting out, 23, 30, 44–45, 72, 76, 125
   countertransference, 93
   suicidal, 48, 65, 66
      clinical example: Patient A, 94
adhesive identification, 108, 124, 143
adhesiveness, 116, 137–138
adhesive pseudo-object relationship, 31, 136–138
adhesive transference, 116
Adler, G., 69, 85
aggressivity, 2, 9–10, 13–18, 22–23, 27, 36, 140
   clinical example: Patient A, 46, 50, 72
   foetal, 2, 9, 23, 32, 118–119
   oral, 17
   prenatal, 16–17, 32–37, 99, 118
   self-directed, 13
ambivalence, 17
Ammon, G., 19, 87, 124
analyst, as placental symbol, 110
anchor, as placental symbol, 104
anorexia, 47
anxiety, persecutory, 13
Anzieu, D., 18–19, 22, 121, 133–134, 137, 143
aquatic ferns, as placental symbol, 105
Aray, C., 110
archaic object-love, 7
art, 111
asthma, 121
attachment, 52, 104, 128
   umbilical, 129

attacks on linking, 84
autism, 19, 22, 31, 96–97, 131, 134–136, 138, 143
autistic–contiguous position, 28, 135–136, 138, 143
autistic disorders, 31
auxiliary ego, 70, 92–94

Balint, A., 35
Balint, M., 7–9, 13, 67, 69, 85, 128, 143
ball and chain, as placental symbol, 104
Baranger, M., 123
Baranger, W., 123
barnacles, as placental symbol, 108
barrier, as placental symbol, 90, 107, 124
Bellagamba, H. F., 110
Bergman, A., 12
Bick, E., 22, 124, 137, 143
biological mirroring, 99, 143
Bion, W. R., 14–15, 18, 20–24, 36, 60, 84, 90, 99, 103, 117–118, 127, 135, 142
bipersonal field, 123
birth:
   dream(s), 25, 68
   persecutory, 118
   trauma, 6, 8, 17, 23, 26, 30, 98
Blarer, S., 32
Bleger, J., 143
Blomfield, O. H. D., 14, 25, 32, 36, 96–99, 102, 118, 127
bombs, as placental symbol, 108
Bonaparte, M., 9, 11, 18, 31
boundary, as placental symbol, 110
Bowlby, J., 128, 129
Boyd, J. D., 33

161

brain-ego, 71, 90, 91, 94, 95, 97, 98
Brazilian Association for the Study of Pre- and Perinatal Psychism (ABREP), 6
breast:
    good breast/bad breast dichotomy, 12, 21, 58
    retaliatory, 107
bridge, game of, 112–113
Brownscombe Heller, M., 127
Bryce Boyer, L. B., 128
Buddha, 105
Burger-Piaget, M., 19, 64

Caesarean section, 23, 30, 117
cake, as placental symbol, 27, 104
Caruso, I. A., 32
castration fears, 9
Chasseguet-Smirgel, J., 27–28, 63, 71, 108
Chiesa, M., 84, 85
claustrophobic anxieties, 121
clinical examples:
    Patient A/Miss A, 3, 29, 39–73, 84–85, 93, 104, 113, 115, 117–118, 120–122, 125, 130–131, 136, 140
    Patient C/Miss C, 3, 16, 73–84
cocoon, 23–25, 62, 122, 125, 130–131, 141
    clinical example: Patient A, 49–58, 62
    of idealization (clinical example: Patient A), 52
    transference, 24, 25
conception:
    shock, 10–11, 31
    trauma, 18
consciousness, foetal, 126
container function, maternal, 15
Cooper, A. M., 140, 141
countertransference, 4, 16, 19, 30, 34, 36, 63, 117, 139, 141
    acting out, 93
    of nursing staff (clinical example: Patient A), 57, 64–73
    to prenatally regressed patients (clinical example: Patient A), 64–73
    prepuerperal, 3
    puerperal, 3
Cruz-Roche, R., 143

danger from the sky, as placental symbol, 108
Davies, J., 89
Deacon, A. B., 106
death instinct, 9–10, 13, 17, 19, 21, 26–27
demarcation line, as placental symbol, 110
DeMause, L., 6, 22, 29, 35–36, 84, 102, 113, 120–122, 142
depression, 16, 42, 73, 112, 135
depressive position, 135
Deutsch, H., 14, 137
Devereux, G., 10
diabolical parasitism, 20, 122
Dolto, F., 14
"double" (*Doppelgänger*), as placental symbol, 110
Dowling, T. W., 27, 102, 105
dream(s)/dreaming, 10–11, 14, 27, 30, 37, 54, 102, 112, 119
    birth, 25, 68
    foetal, 21
    symbolism, 96, 103

ego:
    auxiliary, 92–94
    brain-, 71, 90–91, 94–95, 97–98
    development, role of placenta in, 87–100
    foetal, 21, 89, 96
    formation, 96
    -nucleus, unconscious, 19, 87
    placental, 96
    prenatal, 13, 17, 87, 88
    rudimentary, 11–13, 87
    prenatal, 13
Eichenberger, E., 32
Eisenberg, L., 98
Elmhirst, S. Isaacs, 142
Emde, R., 143
Evans, G., 11

Fedor-Freybergh, P. G., 35
Fenichel, O., 87, 90
Ferenczi, S., 5–9, 14, 16
filter, as placental symbol, 107
flying kite, as placental symbol, 104
flying saucer, as placental symbol, 105
Fodor, N., 9–11, 18, 31
foetal aggressivity, 2, 9, 23, 32, 118–119
foetal anoxia, 78

INDEX 163

foetal brain, 88–89
foetal conditioning and "learning", 27
foetal consciousness, 126
foetal cravings, 50, 73, 140
foetal dreaming, 21
foetal ego, 21, 89
foetal libido, 32, 118
foetal-maternal placental junction, 28
foetal narcissism, 119
foetal omnipotence, 16
foetal parasitism, 25
foetal regression, 106
foetal skin, 22, 143
foetal transference, 3, 36, 71
foetus, parasitic aggressivity of, 102
folie à deux, as placental symbol, 109
Fonagy, P., 84–85, 110, 113, 141
Foulkes, S. H., 19
Freud, S., 3, 5–6, 9, 13, 18, 25, 36–37, 87, 89–90, 98, 103, 108–111, 113, 124, 141–142
Freud, W. E., 32
frontier, as placental symbol, 110
Frosh, S., 119
fusion, 1, 73, 91–92, 124, 127
and separateness, 126

Gaddini, E., 137
Garma, A., 14
Gesell, A., 11, 33
Giant, in "Jack and the Beanstalk", as placental symbol, 108
Giard, A., 25, 37
Glover, E., 91, 92
go-between, as placental symbol, 107
good breast/bad breast dichotomy, 12, 21, 58
good womb/bad womb dichotomy, 13, 21, 28, 36, 58
Graber, G. H., 6, 8, 17, 18, 19, 35
grappling iron, as placental symbol, 104
Greenacre, P., 10, 17
grid, as placental symbol, 107
Grof, S., 32
Grotstein, J. S., 20, 60, 99, 122–127, 131, 133
group:
    analysis, 19
    "uterine function" of, 19
Grunberger, B., 14, 23, 32, 97, 99, 118, 119

Guntrip, H., 85

Haesler, W. T., 32
Hahn, R., 98
Hamilton, W. J., 14, 33, 35
Hartmann, H., 87–91
Hau, T. F., 32
Hepper, P. G., 27, 33, 37
heredity, 3, 111, 141
    symbolism of, 111–113
Hochmann, J., 71, 72, 73
Hooker, D., 33
Hugo, V., 122

idealization, 63, 115
    cocoon of (clinical example: Patient A), 52
"identificate", 97
identification, 20, 28, 97, 127, 134
    adhesive, 108, 124, 143
    primary, 20, 126
    projective, 14, 23, 25, 36, 97, 117, 126–127
infantile psychosis, 96
International Association for Prenatal Psychology/Internationale Studiengemeinschaft für Pränatale Psychologie (ISPP), 6, 35
International Society for Prenatal and Perinatal Psychology and Medicine (ISPPM), 6
intra-uterine mental life, 7
introjection, 28, 127
ISPP, 6, 35

Janus, as placental symbol, 106
Janus, L., 32
Joffe, J. M., 33
Joseph, B., 22–23, 48, 125

Kafka, F., 141
Kaplan-Solms, K., 141
Kelsey, D., 11
Khan, M. M. R., 124
Klein, M., 10–14, 17, 21, 27–28, 36, 58, 63, 87, 98, 108–109, 120–121, 127–129, 135, 142–143
Klein, S., 20, 32, 85, 97–98, 102, 116, 118, 128
Kleinman, A., 98
Kohut, H., 125

164 INDEX

Kruse, F., 32

Laibow, R. E., 32
Laing, R. D., 19, 85, 96, 102
Lake, F., 18
Langman, R. J., 90, 99
Langs, R. J., 34, 123
Lawson, A. H., 24
legends, 6, 111
libidinal development, "deglutitive" phase of, 16
libido, foetal, 32, 118
Lietaert Peerbolte, M., 9, 11, 18, 31, 54, 101, 105
life instinct, 9
Liley, A. W., 33
limpet, as placental symbol, 108
linking, attacks on, 84
Little, M., 85
lotus flower, as placental symbol, 105
luggage, as placental symbol, 104

Mahler, M., 12, 14, 22, 96, 99, 124
Maiello, S., 31, 97, 99, 116, 143
Maizels, N., 25, 27
Mancia, M., 21, 138
manic disorders, 16
Mason, A. A., 37, 118, 121–122, 142
mediator, as placental symbol, 106–107
Meltzer, D., 22, 35, 99, 124, 137, 143
memory, protoplasmic, 9
Menninger, K. A., 9–10, 13, 17, 21
mental development, dual-track, Siamese-twin theory of, 60, 125–127
mental life, intra-uterine, 7
metabolizing, 15, 127
middle-man, as placental symbol, 107
Milakovic, I., 16, 79
mirror:
  maternal, 106
  as placental symbol, 100, 106, 132, 133
mirroring, 99, 125, 129, 133–134, 143
  biological, 99, 143
mirroring transference, 132–134
miscarriage, 34, 56–57, 65, 116, 120, 137
Mitrani, J., 4, 31, 116, 124, 135–139, 143
Modell, A. H., 23–25
Money-Kyrle, R., 10
Montagu, A., 33
moon, as placental symbol, 105
Mossman, H. W., 14, 33

mother:
  –foetus relationship, 10
  prenatal, 3, 19, 54, 62, 80, 94, 108, 116–118, 132, 142
  aggressivity against, 13, 32, 35, 102–103,
  analyst as, 25, 42, 50, 70, 84, 100, 110, 116, 128, 130–131, 136
  containing, 15
  hospital as, 57–58, 61, 82, 84, 93–94
  transference, 99
Mott, F. J., 11, 19, 22, 54, 80, 96, 101–102, 104, 143
mushrooms, as placental symbol, 105
myths, 6, 11, 111

narcissism, 97, 130, 131
  foetal, 119
narcissistic envelope, 130
Narcissus, 106, 132
near-death experiences, 48, 125
nose-bleeds (clinical example: Patient A), 49–52

object-love:
  archaic, 7
  primary, 7–9, 13, 35, 67, 143
octopus, as placental symbol, 107
oedipal (genital) symbolism, 108
Oedipus complex, 63, 108
  prenatal roots of, 28
Ogden, T. H., 27–28, 135–138, 143
omnipotence, 137
  foetal, 16
oral aggressivity, 17
O'Shaughnessy, E., 139, 140
Osterweil, E., 30, 33, 36

Page, E. W., 90, 99, 123
parachute, open, as placental symbol, 104
paranoia, 140
paranoid personality, 141
paranoid–schizoid position, 135, 143
parapsychological phenomena, 11
parasitical forms of transference, 14, 15, 18
parasitism, 25, 71–73, 105, 107
  diabolical, 20, 122
Paul, M. I., 13–14, 23–24, 29–30, 32, 36–37, 64, 97–98, 102, 115–118, 122, 124, 127, 142

INDEX   165

penitential transference, 29, 117–118, 142
perinatal transference, 29
perinatal trauma, 29, 37
persecutory anxiety, 13
personality, autistic, "impenetrable", "encapsulated" areas of, 21
Pierce Clark, L., 37
pig-in-the-middle, as placental symbol, 107
Pine, F., 12
Pines, M., 99, 125, 133–134, 143
Piontelli, A., 26–27, 29, 142
placenta, 6, 11–12, 20, 23–25, 32, 34–35, 37, 56–61, 65–66, 70, 75, 115–116, 118, 122–129, 138
    intervillous spaces, 123
    mirror, 90, 100, 106, 125, 132
    poisonous, 120, 122
    reflexive function of, 91
    role of in ego development, 3, 87–100
    unconsciously remembered (clinical example: Patient A), 54, 56, 58
placental dysfunction, 69
placental ego, 71
placental impairment, 92
placental membrane, 90, 99, 106, 110, 123–124
placental parasitism, 25
placental symbolism, 3, 11, 22, 27, 84, 101–114
    list of, 103–110
placental transference, 99
Ployé, P. M., 14, 20, 69, 102, 106, 127
polarity, 17
pollution, as placental symbol, 108
Pre- and Perinatal Psychology Association of North America (PPANA), 6
pregnancy, traumatic, 30
prenatal aggressivity, 16–17, 32–37, 99, 118
prenatal ego, 13, 17, 87–88
prenatal levels of transference, 7, 16, 98, 100, 123
prenatal mother, *see* mother, prenatal
prenatal regression, 17, 19, 64–73, 84, 109
    clinical example: Miss A, 51
prenatal self, 20, 96–97, 101, 116, 128
prenatal symbolism, 11, 84, 108

prenatal transference, 32, 65, 97, 99, 132, 133
    clinical example: Patient A, 74
prenatal trauma, 19, 30–32, 102
primal scene, 109
primary identification, 20, 126
primary object-love, 7–9, 13, 35, 67, 143
projection, 24, 28, 107, 127
projective identification, 14, 23, 25, 36, 97, 117, 126–127
protective shield, as placental symbol, 107, 124
protoplasmic memory, 9
psoriasis, 40, 122
psychosis, 96, 99
psychotic breakdowns, 121
punitive superego, 122

Rank, O., 6–7, 36, 70, 110
Raphael-Leff, J., 15
Rascovsky, A., 12, 16–17, 21, 64, 87, 98–99, 118
Rascovsky, M., 16, 98
regression, 19, 53
    disruptive, 69
    foetal, 106
    to mother's womb, 8
    postnatal, 69
    prenatal, 17, 51, 64–73, 84, 109
    therapeutic, 69
renal dialysis, 116–117, 128
research:
    prenatal, 10, 26–27, 30–31, 113
    on twins, 26
resistance, 7, 35
    to prenatal interpretations, 63
retaliatory breast, 107
Roheim, G., 101, 105, 106
Rosenfeld, H., 18, 20, 22, 85, 99
Rosser, R., 128
Rowan, J., 28
Rucker, N., 29, 30
rudimentary prenatal ego, 13
Rushton, D. I., 34

Sarkissoff, J., 32
Sartre, J.-P., 134, 135
Schindler, S., 32
schizophrenic patient, 80
Schusser, G., 33
Scott, W. C. M., 10
Searles, H., 99

Segal, H., 80, 82, 99, 119–120
self, prenatal, 20, 96–97, 101, 116, 128
separateness, 126–127, 137
   and fusion, 126
Share, L., 24, 30, 33, 37, 64, 102
sieve, as placental symbol, 107
Simmel, E., 7, 66, 98
skin:
   -ego, 18, 22, 134
   superego, 121, 122
Sohn, L., 97, 99
Solms, M., 141
Sontag, L. W., 33
spider(s), 37
   -mother, 27
   symbolism, 27, 104, 107
Spillius, E. B., 133
spinning top, as placental symbol, 105
splitting, 17
sponge, as placental symbol, 105
Steiner, R., 32
suicidal acting out, 48, 65–66, 94
suicide, 35, 42–43
   attempt (clinical example: Patient A), 39–40, 93, 125
superego, 121–122
   penitential, 29
   persecutory "eye" of, 122
   punitive, 122
   severe, 117
   skin, 121–122
   surrounding, suffocating, crushing, 37, 118, 120, 142
symbiosis, 27, 96, 124
symbol(s)/symbolism:
   dream, 96, 103
   oedipal (genital), 108
   placental, 11, 22, 27, 84, 101–102
      list of, 103–110
   prenatal, 11, 84, 108
   spider, 27
Symington, J., 27
Symington, N., 3, 36–37, 84, 99, 117, 129–131, 133, 141

tension states, chronic, 87
This, B., 14
transference, 1–3, 5–7, 12, 14–27, 30, 33, 70, 73, 102, 107, 110, 112, 128, 135, 139
   adhesive, 116
   cocoon, 23–25
   "diabolical parasitism" of, 20

foetal, 3, 9, 23, 36, 65, 71
   illusion, symbolic, 123–124
   mirroring, 132–134
   parasitical, 14–15, 18
   penitential, 29, 117–118, 142
   perinatal, 29
   persecutory aspects of, 56
   placental, 99
   prenatal, 1, 7, 16, 23, 32, 65, 74, 97–100, 123, 132–133
      mother, 99
   prenatal underscoring of, clinical example, 40–64
   very primitive levels of, oral mechanisms in, 22
trauma:
   perinatal, 29, 37
   prenatal, 19, 30–32, 102
"Trauma der Zeugung", 18
tree, as placental symbol, 27, 102, 105, 108–109
Tustin, F., 22, 31, 96–97, 136–137
twins, 26, 37
   research on, 26

UFO abduction by extraterrestrials, 24
Ulysses, 12
umbrella, open, as placental symbol, 104
unbewusste Ich-Kern, 19, 87
Unlusterlebnisse, 18
Urhass, 17

Van Den Bergh, B. R. H., 33
Verny, T., 6, 22, 99
Veszy-Wagner, L., 15
Vogel, V., 35

wheel, as placental symbol, 105
Whyte, R., 28, 36, 127
Wilheim, J., 6, 9, 31
Wilson, A. R., 85
Winick, M., 92, 103
Winnicott, D. W., 10, 35, 85, 129, 137
"Wolf Man", 108–109
womb:
   good/bad, dichotomy, 13, 21, 28, 36, 58
   -mother, 20, 62, 126–127
   return to, 25–28
Wright, K., 134–135

Yorke, C., 98